COMPETING in Japan

COMPETING in Japan

P. Reed Maurer

The Japan Times

First edition, November 1989
All rights reserved.
Copyright © 1989 by P. Reed Maurer.
Cover art by Hamilton Kumiko.
This book may not be reproduced in whole or in part, by photocopy, mimeograph,
or any other means, without permission.
For information, write: The Japan Times, Ltd.
5-4, Shibaura 4-chome, Minato-ku, Tokyo 108, Japan.

ISBN 4-7890-0486-4

Published in Japan by The Japan Times, Ltd.

This and many other fine books on Japan and the Japanese culture and language are published by The Japan Times, Ltd. located at 5-4, Shibaura 4-chome, Minato-ku, Tokyo 108, Japan.

PRINTED IN JAPAN

This book is dedicated to the memory of
Ambassador Nobuhiko Ushiba,
an insider who helped this outsider into Japan

CONTENTS

Preface ix

I. The Door Is Open 1
Chapter 1 Success Is Not Guaranteed, Nor Denied 3
Chapter 2 Pushing On an Open Door 8
Chapter 3 Surviving, Not Yet Winning 15
Chapter 4 Win Friends and Succeed in Japan 24
Chapter 5 God Is (Somewhere) in the Numbers 32

II. Japanese Management—a Myth? 41
Chapter 6 The Uniqueness of Japanese Management More Fiction Than Fact 43
Chapter 7 The Japanese Competitor—Samurai or Wimp? .. 54
Chapter 8 Japanese Company Employees 65
Chapter 9 Half-a-Lifetime Employment 74
Chapter 10 The Japanese Health Insurance System 84

III. Japan Beginning to License Out 93
Chapter 11 R&D Breakout 95
Chapter 12 The Co-development/Co-marketing Boom 106
Chapter 13 Successful Licensing in Japan or, Is the Game Over? 114

IV. Competing in Japan 125
Chapter 14 Pharmaceutical Wholesaling—Life in the Fast Lane 127
Chapter 15 The Joint Venture—Going, Going, Gone 140
Chapter 16 Japanese Companies as International Competitors . 147
Chapter 17 Fundamentals Apply, As Time Goes By 155
Chapter 18 High-Tech U.S. Firms Can Compete 165

Bibliography 169
Index 170

Preface

A BOOK IS BORN

My adviser in graduate school, an embryology professor who wrote the seminal book in his field, once told me Mother Nature knew what she was doing by designing human pregnancy to last nine months. "It takes that long for humans to prepare for the output." The god of would-be authors was even more cautious. Writing a book is a time-consuming process, getting it published is unbearable labor, and the final product is as much a relief as it is a jooy to behold.

I was not prepared for these emotions in early 1987 when I started writing short articles on various aspects of the Japanese pharmaceutical market. It was simply a way to get seventeen years of experience in this market off my back. As the Pharmaceutical Manufacturers Association Japan Representative, I included these articles in newsletters which were periodically sent to American pharmaceutical company managers. Initially, therefore, the material was intended for an American audience.

However, it wasn't long before various Japanese trade magazines asked if they could publish specific articles. For example, I did one piece on the changes occurring in pharmaceutical wholesaling. My friends at the Japan Pharmaceutical Wholesalers Association published this article in their monthly magazine. Much of the same material is presented in Chapter 14 because the distribution system in Japan is a key element for reaching customers of high-tech products.

Late in 1987 Mr. Shunichi Ando, the editor and publisher of *Drug Magazine*, expressed his interest in publishing an article each month for the entire year of 1988. Mr. Ando is a brusque character, both loved and feared in pharmaceutical circles. He minces no words, is a real entrepreneur, and belies many myths about Japanese management practices. Under his rough

PREFACE

exterior is a heart of gold. On several occasions he invited my wife and me to dinner and we established a close personal as well as business relationship.

Drug Magazine is a Japanese-language publication. I do not write Japanese. What made the entire exercise possible was the incredible talent of Mr. Jiro Hayashi. Jiro is a longtime personal friend. We first met in 1976 when I left the Eli Lilly Company in Kobe and joined Merck & Co., Inc. in Tokyo. Later we became business friends, and now he is very active in PMA activities and performs a critical role in the Lederle/Takeda joint-venture, Nihon Lederle.

Jiro has had an interest in languages for a lifetime. His English is fluent. He studied Chinese in college. He did not simply interpret my English, he made it come alive in Japanese. Of course, he is intimately familiar with the pharmaceutical industry, both Japanese and foreign, and was the perfect collaborator for the *Drug Magazine* series as well as the book. I cannot thank him enough for his untiring efforts and enthusiasm for this project.

At about the same time in 1987, Business Tokyo expressed an interest in the articles for their monthly English language magazine. They published six articles in 1988 and I continue to get comments from their readers both inside and outside Japan.

In early 1988, Dr. James C. Abegglen, Professor and Director of the Graduate School of Comparative Culture, Sophia University, and Chief Executive Officer, Asia Advisory Service K.K. recommended putting the articles into book format. This was a difficult challenge because conversion of a series of articles into a book actually requires a complete rewriting of the material to make it a comprehensive, readable package.

Furthermore, the subject matter was primarily related to the pharmaceutical industry. While those of us who work in that industry consider it important, it is small in comparison with other high-tech industries. The sales of IBM alone are larger than those of the entire U.S. pharmaceutical industry. Therefore, the basic premise had to relate to a broader cross section of high-tech industries in order that the book would appeal to a wider public audience.

In retrospect, I feel satisfied with the effort to tie the separate articles

A BOOK IS BORN

together and the premise that my experience in the pharmaceutical industry would provide valuable lessons for others. The pharmaceutical industry may be small but I believe the experiences of competing in this knowledge-intensive industry are instructive for those who operate in fields of emerging technology.

After completing the manuscript it was necessary to find a publisher who would also agree with the premise that my message would appeal to an audience of lay readers. It was my great fortune in June 1989 to meet Mr. M. Ishida, chief editor of the publications department of the Japan Times. This book has been measurably improved by his editing and attention to detail. Particularly appreciated are the changes which made the contents of the book understandable to a reader unfamiliar with the technical jargon of the pharmaceutical industry.

Writing invariably tells you as much about yourself as you tell others. Often it exposed how little I knew, or conversely, how much more I would like to know. This is both exhilarating and humiliating. These highs and lows, as well as the experience of creating, are addictive. It is my sincere wish that readers of this book will experience the same thrill in discovering the real Japan.

My own education in this regard was considerably enhanced by knowing and working with former Ambassador Nobuhiko Ushiba, to whom the book is humbly dedicated. It is not an exaggeration to say that Mr. Ushiba, both in government and in his personal life, did more to enhance the U.S./Japan bilateral relationship than any other single Japanese citizen in the last 30 years.

Our relationship began when he consented to act as an adviser to the Merck Company. His advice was invaluable when we contemplated, then implemented, a strategy to substantially increase the Merck presence in Japan. This began with the buildup of our joint venture, Nippon Merck Banyu, and reached a crescendo with the simultaneous purchase of both the Banyu and Torii pharmaceutical companies.

Beyond his personal commitment to assist us in these endeavors, he encouraged other outstanding Japanese leaders to meet with Merck executives to review our Japan strategy. Included in our meetings were a governor of

PREFACE

the Bank of Japan, a well-known industrialist, and a former vice minister of the Japanese Ministry of Health and Welfare. These men were willing to give their time, not because of their love for Merck, but because of their respect and admiration for Mr. Ushiba.

Our relationship transcended business-related matters. Mr. and Mrs. Ushiba consented to act as go-betweens in my marriage to Miss Yuko Arai. In his usual style, he was not content to play a passive role, but wanted to talk with Yuko's family and offer very pertinent advice. Although his health was failing from an insidious cancer he presided over our wedding in June 1984 with dignity and strength.

His passing was a great loss to Japan. As a "wise man," he guided our two countries through a number of difficult times. His interests went beyond national boundaries. His service as a government employee was untarnished. It remains my pleasure today to meet with Mrs. Ushiba on a regular basis to talk and have her get to know our two daughters. If this book, in a small way, contributes toward better relations between our two countries I know Mr. Ushiba would be satisfied and proud of the effort.

My purpose in writing the book was to encourage American businessmen to take a positive view of the Japanese market. Many U.S. executives are inhibited by myths about Japan and are not facing present-day realities. Those who recognized the dynamic changes and committed resources to exploit market opportunities have been very successful.

As I write this, it is possible to see from my office window the Kodak advertising blimp hovering in the skies over Tokyo. Just a few years ago it was difficult to be aware of Kodak in Japan because Fuji Photo Film was everywhere. Now Kodak has elected to become a major player in Fuji's back yard. We need more of these aggressive actions by a broader representative sample of American companies.

The question arises, "Why was the book first published in Japanese for a Japanese audience?" One general answer is the intense interest the Japanese have in what other people think about them. Books by foreigners about Japan, its people, and business systems have sold many more copies in Japanese translation than in the original English. However, I believe there are three specific reasons why the book was published in Japanese.

A BOOK IS BORN

First is the obvious fact that thousands of Japanese now work for American companies. For example, American pharmaceutical firms in Japan employ approximately 14,000 Japanese, which equates to almost 10 percent of the people working in the pharmaceutical industry. These people need to convince their corporate owners to consistently maintain a major commitment of time, money, and talent to developing their businesses in Japan. Often, Japanese managers do not articulate their needs in a manner which permits the executives to compete positively with other demands on the corporation.

These people must begin to look at their problems and opportunities through the eyes of their Western colleagues. It is not enough to say Japan is different. Few corporate executives in the U.S. have lived and worked in Japan. Cultural mores are unfamiliar, and the language is usually beyond comprehension. Having an interpreter will not get the job done. Nor does it help to portray the market in mysterious terms and vague generalities.

This book attempts to separate fact from fiction and myth from reality. If it provides ammunition to sway corporate opinion it will be good for both sides. Japanese employees of American firms have an opportunity to combine the strengths of American and Japanese management practices to create a business culture different, but better than, either. "When in Rome do as the Romans do" may have been good policy in ancient times, but today we can combine the best of both worlds.

Secondly, how American companies compete in Japan is of interest to local businessmen. Many believe that foreign companies cannot hire good people, or could not understand how to motivate Japanese employees. While hiding behind these assumptions, American competitors were not considered a threat in Japan.

Many Japanese management practices are demotivating to young people who are not content to carry the bags of their superiors for half a lifetime. Innovation is becoming a necessity for growth. Creating, as opposed to buying, technology is a prerequisite for success in today's emerging markets. Recognizing how American companies are competing successfully in Japan can stimulate an audit of current procedures, lead to experimentation with new ideas, and force change in a bloated, self-satisfied bureaucracy.

PREFACE

Thirdly, most Japanese pharmaceutical companies have not yet established a significant presence in markets outside Japan. American companies have made many mistakes in establishing viable businesses in Japan, but through this process many valuable lessons have been learned. This book discusses many of these situations.

Learning from the mistakes of others has been a Japanese competitive weapon. Often this was most evident in the "hardware" aspects of production and quality control. Managing the "software" of a foreign business will be a new challenge. America as a market is as foreign to Japanese as Japan is to most Americans. Managers in Japan will benefit from understanding the learning process of entering this market from the outside, as they will do in entering the American market.

In writing this book I have primarily relied upon my own experiences, which were pleasurably and painfully learned since arriving here in 1970. It has been my privilege to have had many patient and understanding Japanese colleagues. It is not possible to name them all but their influence is an integral part of the ideas put forth in this book. I do not believe for a minute that my education is complete, there is still much to learn. In fact, I am certain that what I know about Japan is far outweighed by what is yet to be learned.

But I am lucky. My two young daughters are products of two cultures. Learning through their eyes will be a source of continuing stimulation. They will have a perspective denied to those of us who were born and raised on one or the other side of the Pacific Ocean. They are, as I am quick to remind others, not halves, but doubles. That characteristic may be immensely valuable in their lifetime. Our businesses may also benefit from creating doubles as opposed to half of yours and half of mine to make a whole. There is real synergy from combining the best of both our systems. Those who learn how to do it will make measurable positive contributions to the society in which we live.

Tokyo
July 1989

I

The Door Is Open

Chapter 1

SUCCESS IS NOT GUARANTEED, NOR DENIED

The experience of American firms in Japan's high-technology markets is not comforting. Windows of opportunity open, then close rapidly as Japanese competitors clobber the originators. Losers sulk and cry for government intervention to eliminate unfair trading practices and perceptions of a closed market. Success is not guaranteed, but neither is it denied. Fundamental business strategies do work in Japan but foreign managers apply them sporadically and without passion. This is not the minor leagues.

As an American businessman it does not give me a great deal of comfort to know that Coca-Cola and Schick razors are No. 1 in their respective markets in Japan. Nor does it give me satisfaction to see my government utilize its influence to force the Japanese to buy more oranges or beef. McDonald's and Domino's Pizza may be great success stories but they don't prove American businessmen have learned to compete in Japan where it really counts.

The U.S. position toward Japan is contradictory. Politicians in Washington publicize the smashing of a Japanese radio and call for curbs on investment in U.S. real estate. Meanwhile, at last count, 39 states have set up offices in Tokyo to lure Japanese investment by means of an array of incentives. Americans strongly urge the Japanese to spend more on defense while the average Japanese does not want to repeat the mistakes of the militaristic past.

Some claim the Japanese work too hard and save too much, while criticizing the lack of a work ethic and the consumer-driven society in the U.S. Managers would like U.S. workers to be more like the Japanese but do not want to emulate their narrow wage differentials between workers and managers. Americans appear to want to have their cake and eat it too.

The U.S. has technology that is unsurpassed. We outspend and outman the Japanese research establishment by a factor of 3 to 1. Japanese-born Nobel Prize winners prefer to work in U.S. laboratories where they can express their creativity. Yet the fruits of U.S. research often fail to achieve sales in Japan commensurate with their utility. These are not failures of U.S. research or of an inability to stay on the cutting edge of technology. It is a failure of American businessmen to exploit new markets and keep out competitors who follow.

During 19 years in Japan, I have watched with chagrin as U.S. technological leads opened windows of opportunity into the Japanese market, only to be pushed closed by competitors who simply applied basic business fundamentals in a more effective manner. These failures not only result in an opportunity-cost of lost sales in Japan, they threaten the American firm's competitive position in international markets.

U.S. businessmen cannot blame their research personnel. They cannot hide behind accusations of discrimination by Japanese government officials. There are, of course, infamous stories of efforts to keep out certain products, like metal baseball bats. These practices should be stopped. But the future of the U.S. as a competitive nation will not be determined by baseball bat sales.

We had and still have better research. More than ever before, new ideas originate in America. Japan has tremendous capabilities in development, but the basic U.S. research strength is unmatched. U.S. firms are not beaten in the laboratory and are not losing customers because some super-regulatory authority is restricting the availability of U.S. products.

U.S. executives need to take a hard look at what it takes to compete in Japan. I am not talking about what it takes to compete against the

SUCCESS IS NOT GUARANTEED, NOR DENIED

Japanese, a favorite phrase which says virtually nothing. Japanese competitors are not all alike. There are great Japanese companies that are well-managed, aggressive, and overpowering. There are also companies with incompetent management, weak employees, and poor competitive positions. Competing in Japan, not with Japan, is the theme of this book.

A second theme relates to competition in a specific high-technology industrial sector, namely pharmaceutical products, which share many characteristics of other high-technology sectors. The pharmaceutical industry is driven by research, not production. Employees are concentrated in product discovery, development, and sales operations. Their products are marketed worldwide but the Japanese, U.S., and European markets are the key strategic areas. Manufacturing operations are not pollution, energy, or labor intensive. The "software" of the business is more important than the "hardware." Brains count more than bricks and mortar.

In virtually all high-technology product sectors, the Japanese market is second only to the United States. Pharmaceutical products are no exception. Furthermore, as in other high-technology sectors, Japan is an important source of new products. Therefore, success or failure in Japan impacts on a firm's worldwide sales strategy. A company may succeed in Australia or Brazil, and the incremental results are welcome. However, failure in either of these markets is not critical to the firm. Neither are new products discovered in these markets. On the other hand, Japan is a major league market. You make it here or you cannot consider your firm a true multinational player.

American business should not be content with minor shares of Japan's high-tech markets. A low market share position in a large and rapidly growing market results in a huge opportunity cost. For example, the Japanese pharmaceutical market in 1987 was valued at approximately 26 billion dollars at the manufacturers' selling price level. A 1 percent market share translates into a 260-million-dollar business. The few American companies that have reached or exceeded this level of business have significantly higher shares of the U.S. and European markets for the same products that they market in Japan.

Research expenses to discover and develop a new product today are

THE DOOR IS OPEN

estimated to exceed 120 million dollars. Sales of current products fund research for future products. Not achieving a respectable market share position in Japan restricts a firm's capacity for research, hence a limit is imposed on future growth.

Possibly more damaging in the long-term is the opportunity forfeited to Japanese competitors. Only two American companies were in the list of top twenty pharmaceutical companies in Japan at the end of 1987, and neither were in the top ten. As we will see in a later chapter, Japanese firms are using this favorable position in their home market to fund a productive and innovative research effort. This potential competitive threat would be much less ominous if U.S. firms had a market share position with their products in Japan comparable with what they have achieved outside Japan.

Competing effectively is mandatory, but there is no magic key to success. This book does not offer answers to a lot of "how to" questions. It does not offer a psychological or sociological analysis of the Japanese. The longer you stay in Japan the more difficult it is to generalize about the Japanese. The message here is simply that fundamentals work in Japan just as they work anywhere else — if applied consistently and with an extraordinary amount of passion.

Japanese businessmen are not a new breed of supermen. In the high-technology area, they have often succeeded because we forfeited the game. We didn't show up. At times we showed up with a second-string team. At other tines, we seemed more interested in complaining about the rules than in playing the game. Sometimes we thought we had the game won before it was finished.

Of course, competing in Japan is not a game. It is a process of satisfying a demanding customer who has more than one option to satisfy his needs. It is a process of selecting the best people and motivating them to accomplish extraordinary goals. It means refreshing product portfolios with a stream of new products. It means giving local managers visibility and autonomy to deal with the unique characteristics of the market. In short, it means carrying out fundamental business practices better than the competition.

Success in any business is exhilarating, not to mention profitable. In

SUCCESS IS NOT GUARANTEED, NOR DENIED

Japan, you can be ecstatic at success because you know you have beaten some of the best. Rewards in Japan's lucrative market are potentially huge. Conversely, failure is devastating and jeopardizes worldwide competitive positions. To borrow an old phrase, if you make it here, you can make it anywhere.

Chapter 2

PUSHING ON AN OPEN DOOR

> *American high-tech companies contemplating entry or expansion strategies in Japan must first eliminate the "You cannot do that in Japan" syndrome. Restrictions once limited options. Today, externally imposed barriers are not a factor. Successful companies have proved the viability of a range of alternatives. Limitations are often self-imposed through organizational structure, a minor-league commitment to a major-league market, and lack of experience in dealing with Japanese competition. The door is open.*

With many high-tech products, American firms will face, or are facing, competition from the Japanese in markets outside Japan. How to respond is a learning experience best had in Japan. Waiting until the Japanese are in your home market may be too late.

A first step in this process is to fully recognize that the door to Japan is open. The opportunity for success is not primarily limited by government regulations, culture, or business practices. To premise a firm's future on a preconceived notion of what you cannot do in Japan is pushing on an open door.

Consideration of entry strategies or opportunities for growth in Japan's high-technology markets need not be constrained by out-of-date notions of barriers to foreign firms. The options are not limited by government regulations. The characteristics of this market are positive for the research-intensive, innovative, multinational firm. Nevertheless, foreign management often labors under advice which usually begins, "You cannot do that in Japan." Continuation of policy analysis under this assumption is also akin to pushing on an open door.

The Japanese market is not only large, it has grown rapidly for the last twenty years. This fact is no longer ignored by managers of multinational firms. However, a variety of economic and cultural factors have caused many to take a dim view of the future or to question the viability of proposals to commit resources to this market.

A "wait and see" attitude toward a total commitment in Japan ignores many positive, underlying trends of the market. Government-administered price reductions prompted many managers to question the very viability of the pharmaceutical market during the 1980s. But volume growth was chugging along at double-digit levels. Value growth averaged 5 percent. Sales growth of many Japanese companies significantly exceeded these average rates. In other words, while American managers were wringing their hands over price reductions, their competitors were increasing market share.

Other positive aspects of the pharmaceutical market include:

1. New products are listed in the National Health Insurance (NHI) system four times a year. They clear regulatory review, on average, ten months faster in Japan than in the U.S. New products are not restricted in the market. Almost 14,000 products are available from 442 firms in the NHI price list.

2. The percentage of people over the age of 65 is increasing dramatically. It is now almost 16 percent and expected to grow to almost 24 percent by the year 2020. This segment of the population intensively utilizes health care systems, including drug therapy. For example, in 1986, 25 percent of health care costs were attributed to the over-65 age segment, but they represented only 10 percent of the total population.

3. The Japanese patent system protects products as well or better than any comparable system in the world. Furthermore, since January 1988, Japan has enforced a patent term restoration procedure which extends the

life of patents up to five years, based upon the time required for regulatory review and approval procedures.

4. In Japan there is an infrastructure conducive to the growth of a viable pharmaceutical industry, or any high-tech industry. A quality education system provides high-caliber entry-level employees for research and marketing functions. The cultural bias toward health care generally, and drugs specifically, is very positive.

5. Japanese government policies have been positive for the industry. Other governments have introduced regulations and laws to encourage mandatory licensing, restricted drug lists, incentives for generic prescribing, central purchasing agencies, and restrictions on dispensing by physicians. These policies have not been seriously debated, let alone enacted in Japan. An industry that is innovative, knowledge-intensive, high-tech, and internationally competitive are the objectives pursued by various government ministries.

6. Physicians and other health care personnel are available to company representatives. The intensity of detailing, or doctor presentations and visits, is very high. New product acceptance is rapid and conversion to newer products is innovative rather than conservative.

7. Virtually every person in Japan has access to medical care and is covered by some form of insurance. Co-pay schemes take a small proportion of financial resources from an increasingly affluent population. The consumer expects to receive drug therapy, and generally follows the physician's instructions explicitly.

All of these underlying factors should continue into the foreseeable future. They are positive and are in no apparent danger of being reversed by changes in either political or economic policy. However, the Japanese environment is not totally positive for American pharmaceutical firms. There are problems and challenges.

The market size is overvalued because it is measured at the National Health Insurance (NHI) price level, which is the price at which the government reimburses physicians and hospitals for the drugs they dispense to patients. Substantial discounts from the reimbursement price are demanded from manufacturers to cover operating costs and generate income to

PUSHING ON AN OPEN DOOR

"make up" for the relatively low technical fees the physicians receive for their diagnostic and "software" functions. Therefore, a sizable percentage of funds allocated for drug purchases are in reality "leaked" to cover other costs. Although the percentage varies by product category, on average it is reported to be 24 percent.

The system of drug price surveys and revisions invariably results in a downward spiral of reimbursement prices. The manufacturer with the best intentions has little leverage to avoid discounting, followed by a price revision. In the past, these revisions were capricious as partial price revisions were made at irregular intervals. The manufacturer did not know what products would be revised, or when they would be revised.

Another challenge is the diversity of drug purchasers. The hospital market is about equal in size to the general practitioner or private clinic market. This fact, coupled with the high frequency of detailing, demands a sizable marketing force for complete coverage. Major companies employ between 1,000 and 1,500 medical representatives to cover a geographical territory not much bigger than California. Foreign firms have not matched their Japanese competitors in the size and possibly the quality of their sales forces.

Pharmaceuticals in Japan are primarily distributed through wholesalers. This is not a unique marketing challenge, but again, it is diverse. No single wholesaler has nationwide distribution. There are over 400 wholesalers in the Japan Pharmaceutical Wholesalers Association and literally hundreds of others are engaged in the business. They have the day-to-day responsibility for price negotiations and collection of money. Controlling the distribution of drugs requires a commitment of manpower to nurturing close business relationships with wholesalers.

With over 1,300 pharmaceutical firms, the market is intensely competitive. The sales concentration ratio is very low compared with other industries, with ten leading companies accounting for less than 39 percent of the market. Given the nature of the competition and the availability and rapid acceptance of new drugs, it is not surprising to note short product life cycles. A firm must have the marketing muscle and critical mass to secure market share quickly and sustain it in the face of many competitors.

THE DOOR IS OPEN

Options

As events over the past fifteen years have proved, no particular entry or growth strategy is automatically precluded for American firms. There are many roads to success. American companies have proved it is possible to operate in Japan across a spectrum of options:

1. License out technology and marketing rights to a Japanese company strong enough to adequately develop, register, promote, and distribute new products.
2. Work with Japanese companies as in No. 1 above but supplement their activities with 100 percent-owned development, promotion, and/or manufacturing capabilities.
3. Enter a joint venture in a variety of equity and sharing-of-labor arrangements.
4. Establish and build a 100-percent-owned company, capable of conducting everything from research and development (R&D) to distribution.
5. A merger and/or acquisition strategy.
6. A combination of the above.

One option pursued aggressively in recent years is the establishment of a research laboratory in Japan that facilitates contact with research personnel in both industrial and academic laboratories. A presence at the basic research level is a prerequisite for participating in the new product discovery process which is now receiving so much attention in Japan.

Other options include co-development and co-marketing agreements. Typically, each party considers this a win/win proposition since it can lead to a flow of new products and greater coverage of the market. It also spreads the risks of escalating product development expenses.

Current Situation

Japanese-origin products and Japanese companies dominate the pharmaceutical market. In 1987, sixteen of the top twenty companies were wholly-owned Japanese firms. U.S. companies probably control between 8 percent

PUSHING ON AN OPEN DOOR

and 10 percent of sales and employ approximately 10 percent of the total pharmaceutical work force, a significant presence but hardly commensurate with their presence elsewhere in the world.

Some have explained away this relatively poor competitive performance as due to obstacles deliberately put into place by the Japanese government, or to a "closed" system. They make attempts to prove discrimination in matters of price and product approvals. They spend an enormous amount of management time pushing against a door they believe is closed.

The answer, as seen by others, is more rational and can be understood in common business terms. Three factors have been responsible for the poor competitive performance of American pharmaceutical firms:

1. The market, until the mid-1970s, was closed in the sense that it limited entry only to joint ventures. Although these restrictions were lifted over ten years ago, managers continue to believe their only option is to associate themselves with a Japanese company. This strategy precludes allowing operating personnel to have real-world contacts with customers and government authorities. They become slaves to information given by their Japanese partner. Thus, the American company has no contact with the consumer and does not build relationships with physicians, wholesalers, professors and government officials. Therefore, alternative options cannot be evaluated realistically and do not appear either feasible or cost-effective as opposed to a business as usual approach.

2. Success in a major-league market does not result from a minor-league commitment of resources. Japan is often given no more management time than other subsidiaries. It is commonly organized as part of a "Far East Region," lumped together with other countries. The head of Japan operations reports to an area vice president who reports to a group vice president or to the president of international, then to a corporate vice president and maybe, finally, to the chief executive officer (CEO). The head of the U.S. market is typically positioned much closer to the CEO.

3. Japan is the only drug market in the world in which foreign companies face Japanese competition. In America, U.S.-based drug firms

face European competition. In Europe, European firms face formidable U.S. competition. In every other country, they both compete against each other and against small, usually government-protected, local pharmaceutical firms with no significant R&D capacity. In Japan, foreign firms make inadequate competitive responses because of the lack of experience in dealing with Japanese competitors elsewhere in the world.

The Future

American firms are beginning to recognize the need for a Japan presence. By presence, I mean an operational capacity to conduct basic research, develop products, register products, devise and implement marketing plans, manufacture, sell, and distribute products to customers.

A firm's decision whether to conduct these activities through a wholly-owned firm, joint venture, or an acquisition is not the issue. The real issue is a commitment to hands-on management of Japan operations and an organizational structure that brings to top management's attention the specific and often peculiar needs of the Japanese market.

Success in Japan requires a consistent application of time and money. The American firm cannot afford a stop-and-go policy. It must be fully committed to establishing a presence over the long term. The potential rewards are too great to think in any other way.

Chapter 3

SURVIVING, NOT YET WINNING

> *Many American high-tech firms have been in Japan for a generation. They had a monopoly on technology. They have money and resources far in excess of their Japanese competitors. Yet they do not dominate the market and their products lag behind sales achieved in other countries. They make money but may have missed the golden ring. Some are making a determined effort to succeed, and will. For many, the window of opportunity is closing fast.*

In March 1970 I lived at the Imperial Hotel in Tokyo for one month. Every day, from 9:00 a.m. to 5:00 p.m., four different Japanese instructors at the Berlitz School were individually pounding elementary Japanese into my head. They called it "total immersion." It was the most difficult mental exercise I had ever been through — not one word of English for four weeks.

The Imperial Hotel had just opened its new building after tearing down the classic Frank Lloyd Wright structure, which had graced the Tokyo landscape through a war and the great Kanto earthquake. Only the wrecker's ball brought down the walls, and in its place stood a modern symbol of Japan's entering a stage of affluence.

In the cavernous lobby, Japanese businessmen would meet their clients,

THE DOOR IS OPEN

discuss contracts, and at the end of an evening on the town, bring their foreign guests "home" to have one final drink and say good night. Observing this ritual was part of my education in Japanese business etiquette.

A repetitive pattern emerged. A clutch of Japanese businessmen would surround the foreign visitor, complimenting his company, products, and understanding of the Japanese way of doing business. It was obvious the foreigner enjoyed the attention, appreciation, and politeness of his hosts. His trip was a success.

Quite suddenly a young lady would appear and join the group, sit next to the visitor, freshen his drink, light his cigarette, and do general housekeeping of the table in front of him. She was known by some of the Japanese and joined in the chorus of praise for the visitor, adding a few references to his personal charm, wit, and handsome face.

A short while later, as if on cue, the Japanese men would say their sayonaras and with deep bows beat a hasty retreat toward the exit. The girl remained and it did not take the visitor long to figure out he had been the recipient of a final present. As the couple made their way to the elevators I tried to visualize the visitor's trip report one week later back in the home office. Would it say anything negative about the Japanese distributor?

Early on I decided not to fall into the trap of seeing only the surface of Japan. I was determined to get to the reality and not the image of this society. This gave me a lot more motivation to study the language and progress beyond "kore wa hon desu" (this is a book). There is no way you can understand people if you cannot speak to them in their own language.

Knowing the Market

Two years before coming to Japan, I attended the Sloan Program at the Stanford Business School for ten months. Over and over again we were told to know our market and know the customer. Case studies exposed company failures that resulted from not doing market research and not staying attuned to customer needs. Success stories drummed home the value of service to the user.

SURVIVING, NOT YET WINNING

Unfortunately, lessons such as those taught at Stanford are often not applied to the Japanese market by American firms. Senior managers do not know how to speak, read or write Japanese. Often, they remain in Japan for only two or three years before rotating back to the home office. Everything they learn about the market is communicated to them through an interpreter, filtering out critical information or relating only a portion of the message.

Japanese staff are often recruited on the basis of their ability to speak English. In many cases, this is the limit of their capability. They know how to relate to Americans but are not respected by Japanese businessmen. Historically, interpreters have not been given very high status. They were a necessary evil after Perry opened the doors to Japan. Like fish out of water, modern-day interpreters demand symbols of rank, title and salary to make their environment palatable. The perks they receive alienate men of similar age working in the same Japanese companies Americans rely upon for information about the market. In time, the English-speaking Japanese employee may become as isolated from the market as his expatriate boss.

At the risk of sounding like a broken record, I repeat that the language barrier is an important issue true of every industry. Language barriers cannot be over-emphasized. For the most part, American managers in Japan are illiterates. No one would seriously consider appointing a man responsible for U.S. operations who could not read, write and speak English. Yet people with no knowledge of Japanese are routinely assigned to manage businesses in Japan. Justifications for this practice are difficult to understand.

Market knowledge also eludes American firms because of the nature of their business structure. Often contact with customers is forfeited to Japanese distributors because it is considered cost-effective and risk-free in the short-term. In the long-term, however, it is very dangerous to be isolated from customers. Correcting this problem is expensive, and once extra people are hired to do the job they cannot be arbitrarily cut back. However, these expenses pale in comparison with the opportunity-cost of not knowing the customer.

Successful American companies have established an enviable position in

Japan by recognizing the problems cited and have applied several long-term, consistent actions to overcome them.
1. Japan operations are afforded a high level of visibility in the corporate hierarchy. This insures senior management attention to the opportunities of the market, and the need for adequate resources to exploit them.
2. Men assigned to work in Japan are given the full support of corporate management, protecting them from inevitable criticism leveled by staff personnel. Home office staff functions rarely employ people who have lived and worked in Japan. Their critical comments are based upon ignorance of effective procedures that get results here.
3. Qualified Japanese are not assigned interpreter roles, they are true partners in the business process. They are trained continuously and offered opportunities to advance into the most senior subsidiary positions. Reserving these slots for expatriates is a fatal error.
4. Managers are committed to serving the customer directly. They recognize that there is no short cut to establishing a sales force in tune with customers' needs. Relegating this responsibility to a third party isolates the firm.
5. Executives recognize that there are many roads to success in Japan. The most important decision is not which road to take. The real decision is to be committed to travel down a road. The common denominator is satisfying a customer.

Knowing the Product

It is currently fashionable to establish a corporate function responsible for the global marketing of products. Many perceive this as a way to strip the international division of power and to centralize marketing decisions. Others see such a corporate policy as a more efficient allocation of marketing resources and a more rational approach to the realities of today's world. The arguments for and against decentralization and centralization will most likely continue beyond our life span.

SURVIVING, NOT YET WINNING

Meanwhile, product development and the implementation of marketing strategies must take into consideration several unique aspects of Japan's users. Companies that develop a product in their home market first, then turn their attention to Japan at the end of that process, waste valuable time. In a worst-case scenario, they must repeat the entire effort in Japan. The philosophy "If it is good enough for the U.S. customer, it should be good enough for the Japanese customer" is certain to cause frustration.

Japan's special requirements must be considered early in the development cycle. There are many examples of product specifications that were suitable for the U.S. market but bombed in Japan. In the pharmaceutical industry, a typical example would be a daily dose too large for the body weight of the average Japanese patient. Getting the attention of R&D people who have no knowledge of Japan can be a source of friction and bruised egos. People in the Japan office must have a strong communication link with headquarters where action can be taken to satisfy regulatory requirements imposed by the Japanese government.

Japanese customers' stringent quality expectations must also be acknowledged. Consistent adherence to rigid specifications is required. Insensitivity to quality results in lost sales. It is very difficult to ship finished products into Japan and meet the quality demanded by Japanese customers. Unfortunately, these demands are often interpreted as barriers, or excuses not to buy foreign products.

One example in my own experience occurred when we were selling an antibiotic feed additive for chickens. The color was expected to be a pale yellow. Sometimes the material was a very dark yellow, at other times it was almost white. The variations were perceived by the customers as differences in potency. Of course, laboratory analyses proved otherwise and we were expected to show the data to our angry customers. This was a complete waste of time and led to confrontations rather than solutions.

The issue came to a head when black particles appeared in some shipments. We were informed they were charred bits of the antibiotic and in no way would hurt the chickens. Our manufacturing colleagues had missed the point — chickens did not buy the antibiotic. People made the purchasing decisions and they wanted a consistent color with no black specks. If we could not deliver it, they would turn to a competitive product, one made in Japan.

Even with a quality product and a development program sensitive to the needs of Japanese regulatory procedures, the battle is not over. Promotional programs cannot be cloned from U.S. manuals and simply translated into Japanese. It takes a strong marketing man in Japan to stand up to the global marketers at headquarters and suggest changes in plans used successfully in the U.S. It is even more difficult for a Japanese marketing man to face down his American colleagues. Sadly, he often demurs and the product promotion falls flat.

Knowing the People

Many Americans come to Japan with good intentions. They try to learn the language and diligently work at understanding the process of getting results. They do not keep one eye open for the next promotion out of Japan. The market is exciting and challenging. Frustrations are minimal compared with the rewards.

As these American businessmen learn more about the environment, it becomes obvious that certain Japanese methods and procedures are not mysterious or designed to confuse outsiders. Japanese methods are used because they work. At this point in their Japan experience, Americans can make the distinction between the image and reality of Japan, and they become effective, moving in and out of difficult situations with relative ease.

Above all, they begin to know their people, rely on them, and trust them. In short, they delegate responsibility and know the limits of their own ability. They completely involve the Japanese staff in setting desirable objectives, then get out of the way. They focus on results rather than the process of getting results.

There remains an ongoing debate as to the value of having a Japanese in the top position of an American subsidiary in Japan. On the one hand, a Japanese has a clear understanding of the Japanese language and culture. On the other hand, Americans more easily grasp home office strategies and

SURVIVING, NOT YET WINNING

goals. Experience has demonstrated that both sides of the argument have merit. The bottom line is the caliber of the person, not his or her nationality.

"Good people are hard to find." This is no more nor less true in Japan. Good people can be recruited and kept within the organization. However, it requires a consistent effort to solicit the good will of professors who recommend companies to students who are prospective employees. Recruiting efforts cannot be made on a stop-and-go basis. A hire this year, no-hire next year policy is certain to fail.

Determination

Innovative technology does not guarantee success in Japan. Competition is fierce and windows of opportunity do not remain open forever. Old technology is like yesterday's news, it rarely sells. Firms with useful products have many options to establish positions of strength. Barriers exist primarily in the minds of management. The problems of entry and expansion are manifold, but the potential payoff is greater than in any other market outside the U.S.

Generally, there are several patterns of success. Firms do not need to reinvent the wheel. We hear more about the problems, but it's only because successful companies do not complain. These companies are busy making money and generally know what does or doesn't work.

Success Comes to Those Who...	Unsuccessful Companies...
1. Know their customer because they have people calling on customers.	1. Relegate customer contact to distributors or joint venture partners.
2. Satisfy their customer by providing him with what he perceives as valuable.	2. Confront their customer with values they believe the customer should appreciate.

THE DOOR IS OPEN

Success Comes to Those Who...	Unsuccessful Companies...
3. Hire qualified people who know how to get a job done.	3. Hire people who know how to talk about the job in English.
4. Support their local management and protect them from the barbs of the uninformed.	4. Believe their home office staff know more than the people living in the market.
5. Develop a product for Japan.	5. Develop a product for the U.S. first, Japan second.
6. Satisfy the quality demands of Japanese consumers.	6. Satisfy internal quality standards first, customer's second.
7. Market a product with a Japanese promotional plan.	7. Market a product in Japan based solely on a global promotional plan.
8. Trust their Japanese employees to get the job done.	8. Dictate how their Japanese employees should do the job.
9. Select the best men to lead the organization.	9. Pick only Japanese to lead under a blanket policy of Japanization.
10. Recruit on a planned, consistent basis.	10. Recruit sporadically.

At the end of the day, successful companies in Japan have one common characteristic — an intense, passionate desire to be competitive in this market. They are not put off by the pessimists or people who know all the reasons why Americans cannot succeed in Japan. They do not fall for short-term advice, and measure results on the basis of sales made last month.

Determination transcends temporary setbacks. Those companies without it find that they are overwhelmed by Japanese competitors that are becoming stronger every day.

SURVIVING, NOT YET WINNING

But the window of opportunity is closing fast. U.S. companies without a substantial presence in Japan may be relegated to small, unsustainable market-share positions. Entry and expansion strategies become more difficult to implement, and the costs associated with these efforts escalate.

If I were to list all of the ideal characteristics of a market, Japan would rank high on the list. How companies succeed or fail here may be indicative of their success worldwide. Understanding how to speak, read and write Japanese is not the only issue. Those companies lacking an understanding of Japan cannot convert technological superiority into market dominance. Without a respectable market position in Japan, firms invite Japanese competition and later must fight these same competitors in other markets. At that time, the outcome of the battle may already have been determined. Therefore, understanding Japan and succeeding in Japan mean an appreciation for competitiveness worldwide.

Recently I returned to the Imperial Hotel to observe the nightly ritual. It has changed. Japanese now drop their foreign guests off at the door, say good night, and are driven off in their chauffeured Toyotas and Nissans.

Chapter 4

WIN FRIENDS AND SUCCEED IN JAPAN

Reach out and ask someone to help. Companies realize it is imperative to succeed in Japan. The difficulties are emphasized. Getting through the maze can be simplified by utilizing outside advisers. Distinguished Japanese business, technical and government people are willing to assist foreign companies. Relationships require time to nurture, are best kept out of the headlines, and monetary reward is not the primary motivation. Successful companies utilize these resources effectively. The process begins by asking.

It is common knowledge among executives with experience in Japan that friendships and being a part of the "old boy" network are necessary prerequisites to doing business successfully. Learning to respect and listen to those friends, however, remains a weak point of U.S. firms in Japan. Edward T. Hall, co-author of *Hidden Differences: Doing Business With the Japanese*, wrote: "American management in the past has been singularly blind to the needs of human beings. Management wants to eliminate the human equation from business. . . . That puts businessmen at a disadvantage overseas because so many businesses are based on human relations and friendship. They say, 'How the hell could you do business by making a friend? What's that got to do with the bottom line?' As it turns out, it has everything to do with it. . . . We're impatient. But all over the world, if

WIN FRIENDS AND SUCCEED IN JAPAN

you have friends, you can do anything. That's how the system works."

In the early 1970s, I was a panel speaker at a program sponsored by the business school of the University of Wisconsin on doing business with the Japanese. My memory of the event does not, unfortunately, include my own remarks, but I do have a vivid memory of a Japanese panelist responsible for establishing a factory for his company in Wisconsin. In an informal conversation, I asked him about his progress.

I was fully prepared to hear about real estate agents, construction firms, zoning boards, bankers and labor practices. What I got was completely different. He began in an enthusiastic manner: "We have set up an advisory panel, to which I have devoted my full attention since arriving in Wisconsin. Our advisers include the governor of Wisconsin, the mayor of the town where we would like to build our factory, and a well-known professor of business from this university. Everyone has been so friendly and cooperative."

Puzzled, I asked, "What will they do?"

His response came quickly. "We want them to be our friends. We want to do business here in a proper manner and be a good employer. Everything is different here and this is our first factory in America. We have outlined our plans to each person and asked for their guidance and support."

I followed the progress of this company and was not surprised that the factory site had been located, construction proceeded smoothly, many more people applied for employment than could possibly be employed, and production was initiated much sooner than originally thought possible. The plant has since been expanded as sales have increased. In fact, we have a bottle of their product in our kitchen in Hawaii. The product is soy sauce and the label boldly states: Brewed by Kikkoman Foods, Inc. in the U.S.A. The back label says: Brewed by Kikkoman Foods, Inc. Walworth, WI 53184 U.S.A. On the side of the bottle is a Good Housekeeping Seal of Approval.

The Kikkoman executive's first priority was not to do "business," it was to make friends. He had confidence in the product and production processes. To him, the key to success was not technology, it was human relations.

THE DOOR IS OPEN

One knee-jerk reaction to this story was to set it aside as another example of U.S., particularly midwestern U.S., hospitality and openness. A cynical reaction was to look for a payoff somewhere along the line. Yet another reaction was to assume assistance like this would not be given to Americans doing business in Japan. "Yes, we are open, they are closed."

My own propensity was to have the latter reaction. In America, everyone is welcome. Anyone can become an American, but you must be born a Japanese to be Japanese. Furthermore, none of my business associates in Japan spoke about Advisory Councils. Sure, the Japanese had their old-boy network, school friends and interlocking business groups. But somehow this was "reserved" for Japanese companies, not American companies.

In America we speak with pride about the friends we have who are not associated with us in the company. Japanese are socially more comfortable around the people they also work with. During my early years in Japan I thought of my business associates as friends in the office, but not friends in my social or personal life. The line was drawn — or so I thought.

The oil shock first changed my attitude toward what I could expect from Japanese friends. Our house was heated by kerosene, which was common practice in those days. Kerosene dealers were definitely in a seller's market, as everyone was hoarding. Price was a secondary issue. What mattered was finding someone willing to deliver enough to keep the tank from running dry.

The oil shock also resulted in limited supplies of toilet paper in Japan. When stores opened, there was an immediate mad rush for the toilet paper section and the shelves were stripped bare in a matter of minutes. People were returning from overseas trips with boxes of toilet paper instead of the usual bottles of Scotch whisky.

The Japanese have always been sensitive to the fact that their island country has few natural resources. In an earlier age, the availability of oil was not a major issue in the lives of ordinary people. However, by the early 1970s oil was the basis of not only light and heat, but many products essential to daily living. Japan is totally dependent upon imported oil and the possibility of being cut off created a sense of real crisis not felt by the average American.

With a family that included two small children, it was not pleasant to contemplate the dual absence of heat and toilet paper. To add to our discomfort, soap powder was also heading for the out-of-stock list. Then, surprisingly, various people began to drop by and offer small quantities of toilet paper and soap. The kerosene man kept the tank full at a very modest increase in price.

Our good fortune turned into somewhat of an embarrassment as we approached surplus capacity. Fortunately, the panic situation returned to normal within a short time and calmness returned to the markets. Upon reflection, it was almost unbelievable how friends had come through and helped our family during this chaotic period.

Business Friends

Friendships made in the business world go beyond making a tour in Japan personally satisfying. They form the basis of trust in the company and the products it has to offer. In Japan's homogeneous society, American companies are outsiders and they must work harder at overcoming preconceived notions of "the devil you know is better than the devil you don't know."

It has been my good fortune to be on the receiving end of good business advice and counsel from Japanese friends, and my experience is not unique. Others have had the same experience and have turned it into concrete, positive results by organizing friends into advisory councils for their companies. But before committing a company to such a corporate strategy, management must be committed on several points:

1. Be prepared to respect and listen to advice. If company executives believe they already have all the answers and simply want help to implement a fully-prepared plan, advisers will feel that the company is wasting their time.
2. Be prepared to build a close working relationship with patience. It

will probably take three to five years of nurturing a mutual level of respect before you have an effective channel of two-way communication.
3. Be prepared to accept advice even though it may cause some painful readjustments in the company's previous plans.
4. Be prepared to sell the firm's strengths and weaknesses. The company name may be a household word in New York but unknown in Tokyo.
5. Be prepared to focus attention on what is the company's single biggest problem in Japan. Not all problems can be solved at one time.
6. Be prepared to do homework as to the most suitable candidates for advisory roles.

Any company can select several areas in which outside advisers may make significant contributions. Much depends on what level of sophistication the firm has achieved in Japan, which is usually a function of time and presence. However, no company knows everything and does everything well. Friendly advice is not a luxury, it is a critical need. There are many areas in which advisers can be useful.

A General Business Advisory Council. Most senior executives of American firms have not lived and worked in Japan. As a result, there is a gap in understanding that causes problems when financial resources are requested for the Japan area. Ignorance often leads to distrust, prompting exhaustive studies and analysis ad nauseam of the Japan plan. A panel of Japanese advisers, who are respected by the home office, can support the commitments of money and thereby introduce a comfort level to an otherwise awkward situation.

General business advisers may be asked to give direction on specific subjects or may be consulted on major strategic policies, macroeconomic, political or social trends in Japan. This sort of "wise men's group" has been used by both the Japanese and American governments and can prove effective for companies.

This type of advisory council should have a limited number of people. For example, a person who had an outstanding career in politics, the foreign service, or a government ministry; a well-known industrialist; a person who had a career in finance, such as banking or securities or the Ministry of Finance; and a person from academia.

A Medical Advisory Council. As a specific example from the pharmaceutical industry, companies in that field doing clinical research in Japan have contact with leading professors on a product-by-product basis. Good reasons exist to establish a more permanent group of leading medical scientists and educators to advise on general trends in medicine. Specific product relationships end when the clinical trial is terminated.

An advisory council can be organized to reflect general areas of medical therapy of interest to the firm, i.e., cardiovascular medicine. Or it can be structured to include only university professors with a variety of interests. It may have permanent members with others brought in to deal with specific subjects, but a leader well respected by his colleagues should be designated.

A Personnel Advisory Council. Perhaps there is no greater challenge to the foreign firm than attracting good people, motivating them, and paying competitive wages and benefits. Having a group of advisers in this area would appear to be logical and critical. Firms that turn to executive recruiters or Japanese business partners for assistance in recruiting may receive biased recommendations.

A Scientific Advisory Council. Some American firms are establishing basic research operations in Japan. Building a facility may be the easiest task in this process. Attracting good people, establishing research themes, interacting with university laboratories and administering the research are perplexing issues.

An advisory group of noted scientists can help to overcome these problems. The group need not be limited to Japanese researchers working in Japan. There are many excellent Japanese specialists working in laboratories outside Japan.

A Public Relations/Political Advisory Council. In the United States, firms consider their liaison with the mass media and government authorities to be of utmost importance. Significant amounts of time and money are expended to monitor the progress and positively influence the outcome of legislation. Good public relations is equally important in Japan.

An advisory council in this area might include a media representative, a former minister or vice minister of a government ministry, an academic familiar with your industry, and a person from an industry association.

The list could go on and on. For example, advisers in manufacturing, marketing, finance, sales training and computer operations. The point is to select your greatest weakness and to get the best possible outside advice in that area.

Advisory Council Procedures

Localize the Process As Much As Possible. There may be good reasons for creating an international board of directors and selecting one Japanese person to represent the firm's interests in Japan. Japanese professors on the faculty of U.S. business schools may offer excellent advice to the home office. A more effective approach, however, is to create advisory councils in Japan and involve local staff in the process.

Generally, potential advisers do not look for publicity as a reward for the relationship with a specific American company. Like any person, an adviser may like a good press, but a low-key approach is considered more professional. Bragging about the fact that so-and-so is a good friend of the company is not good style.

Advisory relationships require constant nurturing if they are to remain productive. Out of sight is out of mind. We always made a point of calling on our advisers at regular intervals, if for no other reason than to pay attention to traditions in Japan such as seasonal greetings. Irregular visits by executives from the home office are not sufficient to maintain a close association and build a basis of trust.

Remuneration should also follow local custom. Be assured your advisers are not helping you for the money, they are doing very well in their current endeavors. They will help for other reasons, not the least of which may be their honest desire to open Japan. Many Japanese are smarting from the criticisms of a perceived closed society, or believe it is time to pay back others for the assistance they received in the past.

WIN FRIENDS AND SUCCEED IN JAPAN

Avoid Stop-and-Go Tactics. Establishing an advisory council may seem like a good idea in year one. By year three it is functioning smoothly. In year five, for whatever reason, the councils are disbanded. In year eight, new management has good reason to reinstate the idea but nothing happens. Word spreads quickly when commitments are not maintained.

Be Honest. If you are sincere in a desire to expand the business in Japan you must be honest with yourself and act accordingly. It does not hurt to ask dumb questions, but listen, listen, listen. If a firm is solely interested in a quick fix or a special favor not accorded to others, advisers will drift silently away. It suddenly becomes "difficult" to get an appointment.

Language and cultural difficulties often lead Americans to believe Japan is the most frustrating market in the world. It can appear to be completely closed if you are on the outside looking in. Successful companies inside Japan do not complain. They actively seek inside help and act upon the advice given.

The importance of being inside a market cannot be over-emphasized. Many American managers live in Japan but are outside their market. Information is essential to dispel outdated notions or preconceptions gleaned from the uninformed. Advisers can help to get beyond the images and myths. Information is not hidden from those who ask for it. The process begins by asking.

Chapter 5

GOD IS (SOMEWHERE) IN THE NUMBERS

> *Government ministries and other organizations spew forth an enormous amount of statistical data regarding the Japanese market and the health and welfare of 122 million Japanese. Most is reported without comment. It would seem everything is counted, at least once. The data are available for all to see, ponder, and wonder what it all means. To businessmen, particularly Americans, these are largely neglected sources of information. The challenge is to separate the wheat from the chaff.*

Studying statistics is probably not what the average person considers a "fun" project, but it is essential in understanding any market. The computer is changing this attitude because a machine can do the mindless number-crunching that previously required so much valuable time. It is a flexible weapon, available to everyone in a variety of boxes, from laptops to mainframes with PCs, micros and minis in between. Computers alone, however, do not make a better product or increase market share, people do that.

The Japanese are particularly fond of detailed statistical analysis. Possibly this can be ascribed to their love for "small is beautiful," living as they do in confined spaces. It may reflect an island mentality or the homogeneous nature of the population. Whatever the reason, it is clear that Japanese at-

GOD IS (SOMEWHERE) IN THE NUMBERS

tention to detail has been a strong competitive weapon in quality control. The secret relates to measuring every possible parameter of performance from beginning to end. Belatedly, American managers are recognizing the value of built-in quality as opposed to the wasteful process of fixing a product at the end of the line or after it is already in the hands of the customer.

Health care in Japan is also measured by a flood of quantitative data. In fact, the Ministry of Health and Welfare has a Statistics and Information Department that is totally dedicated to keeping track of the nation's pulse. Unlike in many other countries, there is a virtual lode of statistical data available through the records maintained for health insurance purposes which virtually covers the entire population. For example, the population of Japan in 1986 was estimated to be 121,672,000 people, 121,241,000 of whom were actually covered by medical insurance.

Every time a person sees a doctor there is a statistical record of the event and the numbers are staggering. In 1986, there were a total of 766,297,000 medical-care bills processed by all types of medical insurance. This works out to an average of 6.3 bills per person per year.

The average Japanese visits a physician at frequent intervals, as indicated by the following statistics. In 1986, there were 2,290,634,000 days of consultation or 19 days per person. That works out to almost three weeks of doctor visits per year per person. The amount of time Japan does not lose to labor strikes in one year it loses waiting to see doctors. To a pharmaceutical marketer, of course, this high frequency of visits will be of interest since doctors have many opportunities to switch medications.

Hospital statistics also indicate a high intensity of usage. In 1987, there were 9,841 hospitals in Japan. On any given day these hospitals treated 3.0 million patients, 57 percent as outpatients. The inpatients totaled 1.3 million. There were 1.58 million beds available so the occupancy rate was over 80 percent. In fact, the occupancy rate for general medical beds was 83.3 percent. When hotels hit this kind of occupancy rate they consider themselves full. In the U.S., at least one-third of all hospital beds are empty each day. One way to keep your house full is to keep the patients (guests) as long as possible. The length of stay in general medical beds in 1987 was

THE DOOR IS OPEN

thirty-nine days, five times longer than in the U.S. Psychiatric beds were occupied, on average, for 522 days, a full year and a half.

Much has been written about the cost-effectiveness of drugs in the U.S. as related to reducing the hospital stay. This type of data is utilized for promotional purposes in a very effective manner. Does it sell in Japan? Pneumonia patients in Japan spend three weeks in the hospital. The effectiveness of an antibiotic in resolving the disease is most likely apparent in three to five days. If one antibiotic works faster than a competitor's by one or two days, who will notice during a three-week hospital stay? The response rate to drug therapy is not a major issue. Other factors influence the length of stay in Japan and may be dealt with as the government exerts more pressure to cut hospital costs.

In the data given above, hospitals are defined as medical care institutions with twenty beds or more. A clinic is a medical care institution with fewer than twenty beds or without beds. In 1987, there were 79,369 clinics in Japan with 277,958 beds. Adding all this together requires one more piece of information, i.e., the number of estimated patients per day. In a 1987 survey, the number of such patients was over 8 million, 82 percent of whom were outpatients. There were 183,000 physicians, so each physician saw forty-four patients a day. It is remarkable that any physician has time to see detailmen (pharmaceutical company sales representatives).

In 1986, there were 42,305 detailmen in Japan, or one rep for every four doctors. There is a lot of competition for the doctor's time. But there is another side to the coin. Assume a pharmaceutical company has 600 reps. Given the data above, each rep would have in his territory: 305 doctors, sixteen hospitals, 132 clinics, 2,653 beds, and 13,449 patients per day.

With these numbers, the frequency of doctor visits, the competition for time in the doctor's office, and the fact that most pharmaceutical companies have less than 600 reps, it is clear that some real planning must be done to target physicians and make effective use of the sales force. One company cannot cover the entire market.

GOD IS (SOMEWHERE) IN THE NUMBERS

Vital Statistics in a Lighter Vein

The Ministry of Health and Welfare does not publish statistics to humor people. Health is a serious business. Yet some data can be interpreted in a less than vitally serious manner.

For example, assume your company was hiring men and women college graduates in 1975 and 1987. On average, 21-year-old males in 1987 were 5.1 cm. taller and 3.7 kg. heavier than in 1975. Females in 1987 were 1.8 cm. taller and 1.0 kg. heavier than those in 1975. Certainly the notion of short and petite no longer applies to the young people in Japan.

In 1960, male college graduates entering companies could rarely expect to live beyond age 49. In 1987, new employees could expect to live to age 56.5. Previous personnel managers did not need to worry about 50-year-old employees and young people moved up the ladder in an orderly fashion. Now a lot of 50-year-old employees are blocking the top of the pyramid.

Data compiled in 1987 indicate that the average Japanese male and female employee gets married at age 28.4 years and 25.7 years respectively. The first child will come 1.1 years later. Physical transfers of males after the age of 30 are going to involve serious family considerations. Female college graduate employees will in many cases be out of the firm after five years.

In 1985, approximately 8 million people were screened in mass examinations for high blood pressure. In the age group from 50 to 59 years, 24.8 percent of men and 18.9 percent of women were found to have high blood pressure, i.e., systolic >160 mm Hg. or diastolic$>$ 95 mm Hg. Therefore, 1.8 million males and 1.4 million females were newly diagnosed as having hypertension. The market for hypertensive drugs is on a fast track.

Life span statistics for men and women are also of interest. In 1987, there were 2 percent more Japanese males than females between the ages of 0 and 4 years. In the age category 65 years and over, females outnumbered males by 45 percent. The years of work and pressure on the job may be taking their toll. Japanese women are the longer-term beneficiaries of Japan's success. Walking three steps behind the old man may not help the ego but it seems to do something for longevity.

Business Statistics

Statistics on the economic performance of Japan are well known and reported in great detail. The human factor statistics are of greater interest. A good place to begin is at the top of an organization. What do companies in Japan and the U.S. consider to be their most important mission? In 1980, a dated but still relevant survey was conducted of 227 U.S. companies listed in the Fortune 500 and 291 Japanese companies listed on the Tokyo Stock Exchange to answer this question. The results are outlined in Table 1, with 1 being the highest priority and 9 the lowest.

TABLE 1

Goal	Ranking U.S.	Ranking Japan
Return on investment	1	2
Raising stock value	2	9
Market share	3	1
Improvement of product portfolio	4	5
Streamlining of production and physical distribution systems	5	4
Ratio of net worth to total assets	6	6
Ratio of new products to total products	7	3
Improvement of corporate image	8	7
Improvement of working conditions	9	8

Compared with American companies, Japanese companies place a very low value on raising the company stock price. On the other hand, they highly evaluate market share position and the number of new products in their line. Companies in Japan cannot reward employees with stock options as they are prohibited from owning their own shares. In other words, "You get what you pay for."

Abegglen and Stalk, in their book *Kaisha, the Japanese Corporation*, reviewed the above data and commented,

GOD IS (SOMEWHERE) IN THE NUMBERS

"Judging from the realities of competition, the elevation by U.S. management of the return on investment goal over the goals of market share and refreshment of the product portfolio would seem to be illogical. In the West, as in Japan, high profits and hence high return on investment come with superior competitive position. Superior competitive position is achieved with good products and maintained with new products, and the measure of superior competitive position is market share. Although there are debates as to how to measure the value of market share, in Japan superior market share means 'I sell more than you where it counts.' If in the pursuit of market share Japanese companies find that they must make certain capital or expense investments to hold or gain share, the investments are made with little regard for the short-term returns of the project. Not making the investment risks a loss of competitive position; the business may well never earn much money."

It is also interesting to note that company presidents in Japan in 1980 earned an after-tax income of only 7.5 times that earned by entry-level employees with a university education. This is a very narrow differential and no doubt creates a sense of togetherness on the company pyramid. A graphic may portray the situation as follows.

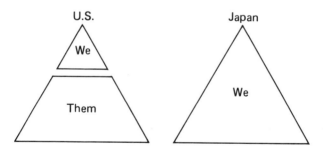

Another indication of the "we" attitude in Japanese companies was illustrated in a survey conducted by the Japan Federation of Employers' Association in 1981. Of 513 companies surveyed, 74.1 percent had board members with experience as union leaders and 16.2 percent of the actual

THE DOOR IS OPEN

board members were, at one time, union leaders. The top level of management is not a restricted club.

A Yankelovich poll of Japanese and American workers in the early 1980s also supports the above assumption. In response to the statement, "I have an inner need to be the best I can, regardless of pay," American workers actually outscored the Japanese. However, when asked "Who would benefit most from an increase in worker productivity?" Ninety-three percent of Japanese workers thought they would benefit, while only 9 percent of American workers felt that way. Tom Peters in his recent book *Thriving on Chaos* analyzes these results as showing that "self-interest probably rules in both countries, but our workers keenly believe that increased productivity and self-interest don't go hand in glove."

In 1983, the Japan Human Relations Association surveyed the suggestion system in Japan. The rate of worker participation was 58.3 percent with an average 14.74 suggestions per worker per year, 75.9 percent of which were adopted by management. Comparable data for the U.S. are available from the U.S. Association of Suggestion Systems for 1978. Only 14 percent of U.S. workers participated and each made 0.15 suggestions per year. Twenty-four percent were adopted by management.

The payoff for a "we" attitude may be the number of days lost (1,000 man-days) to labor disputes. In 1983, Japan lost 507 days, the U.S. 17,461. In 1987, the U.S. number went down to 4,481 while Japan's dropped to 256. These numbers do not relate to what is called the "unionization rate," that is, the ratio of union members to non-agricultural laborers. In 1986-87, the rate in Japan was 27.6, in the U.S. 17.5.

Thomas J. Watson, Sr., the founder of IBM, once said, "There is no saturation point in education." When Admiral Perry sailed into Tokyo Bay in 1857, the Japanese quickly recognized their backwardness in terms of both education and technology. In 1872, long before many countries in Europe, a compulsory education system was introduced in Japan. Education became a national craze. In his book *Japan as No. One: Lessons for America*, Ezra Vogel writes, "If any single factor explains Japanese success, it is the group-directed quest for knowledge."

In 1955, only about 50 percent of Japan's youth entered high school, and

GOD IS (SOMEWHERE) IN THE NUMBERS

less than 10 percent went on to college. By 1980, 93.1 percent of males and 95.4 percent of females finished high school. Japanese students attend school about one-third more than their American counterparts, for 240 days a year compared with 180 days in the U.S.

The same percentage of college-age youths is attending a university in both the U.S. and Japan, but many more Japanese complete their educations. The educational process continues beyond university. In 1987, salaried-worker households in Japan spent 3.5 percent of their disposable monthly income on education as compared with 1.9 percent for medical care and 5.4 percent for clothing and footwear.

A carry-over of this quest for education is seen in Japanese companies where training is legendary, throughout a career. The primary objective is to have well-trained people, but it also sends a "You're important to us" message to each and every individual. As Tom Peters points out in *Thriving on Chaos,* when Nissan Motor moved to Smyrna, Tennessee it spent $63 million ($7 million courtesy of the state of Tennessee) training about 2,000 workers. This amounted to over $30,000 per person, before the plant started operation.

Continuing employee education and training is not cheap, but can provide competitive advantage. American firms would be wise to consider this fact when it comes to the education of their expatriate managers in Japan. Robert C. Christopher, in his book *Second to None—American Companies in Japan,* says 90 percent of the U.S. business people in Japan have never made any attempt to learn Japanese.

However, the tide may be turning. There were 16,000 Japanese-language students in U.S. colleges in 1983, 40 percent more than in 1980. More and more frequently these students are not preparing for an academic career. Their motive for studying Japanese is to have an edge in pursuing a career in business. John Stern, head of the Tokyo office of the American Electronics Association, has said engineers hired by the firms he represents pay a whopping 40 percent premium in salary to those with knowledge of Japanese.

With more of these "new" gaijins (foreigners), statistics prepared by government ministries will no longer go unnoticed by foreign firms operating in Japan. Data alone are not the answer to business success, but they sure help. As John Stern told *Business Week*, "Many representatives of U.S. high-technology companies coming to Japan are 96 percent ignorant of the Japanese market. These companies would rather curse the darkness than light a candle."

Information from advisers, government ministries and trade associations can be utilized to breed a sense of familiarity rather than contempt for Japan within the corporate culture. We do better with what we know than what we do not know. Surprises are never welcomed by corporate managers who want to believe they are on top of the business. They want to be proactive rather than reactive.

Competing effectively in Japan is enhanced through an in-depth knowledge of the market, customer and the people you are competing against. In the next section I take a look at the players — who they are and some of the things they must worry about. Japanese managers and employees have been glamorized in recent years to the point that American managers visiting or living in Japan appear to be intimidated. They try to be more Japanese than the Japanese. Competitive strengths do exist, but weaknesses are also evident to the informed. Knowing the difference is important.

II

Japanese Management—a Myth?

Chapter 6

THE UNIQUENESS OF JAPANESE MANAGEMENT — MORE FICTION THAN FACT

Group harmony, paternalism and seniority are characteristics ascribed to Japanese management that give them competitive advantages unmatched by American firms. A comparative study of Japanese and U.S. pharmaceutical firms demonstrated there is more fiction than fact in this assumption. Study results indicated employee participation in Japanese firms is relatively higher and may focus human resources on quality performance. The consequences of this difference have not yet been tested in managing an international business.

Depending upon which management book has been "hot" during the past ten years, a variety of factors have been cited for Japanese competitive advantages unmatched by American firms. The list of unique Japanese management features appears to be limited only by the amount of time and money observers have to study in Japan. Recently, an impressive list was sent to me by a California professor. It included:
1. Development of strong achievement/performance organizational cultures.
2. Consensus decision making.
3. Commitment/loyalty between organization and participants.
4. Flexible, less specialized managerial systems.
5. Emphasis on group processes/team building.

JAPANESE MANAGEMENT—A MYTH?

6. Integration of technology with social system as illustrated by quality control circles.
7. Strong emphasis on engineering and technical training and applied product and process research.

Those businessmen who have been in Japan longer than the usual three-year tour have sensed there may be more fiction than fact to many of the assumptions made by business publications. A popular story conveys the message.

Three men, a German, a Japanese, and an American, were placed in front of a firing squad to meet their ultimate fates. Before the order to fire was given, each was permitted a final statement. The German said, "I want to tell the world about the importance of discipline and order in our lives." Before the Japanese could speak, the American said, "I want to be shot first so I will not have to listen to another lecture on the uniqueness of Japanese management practices."

Fortunately, in the midst of my own frustration over this barrage of Japanese competitive advantages, my wife conducted a comparative study of in-house company magazines published by Japanese and American pharmaceutical companies. The study was conducted as part of her master's thesis at the University of Hawaii. Since she is totally fluent in both Japanese and English, the analysis was conducted without intermediate translation, which often misses certain nuances of the original documents.

Out of the long list of factors considered uniquely Japanese, she selected group harmony, paternalism and seniority as variables in an intensive-content analysis with rigidly controlled parameters. The rest of this chapter is devoted to reporting her results.

Group Harmony and Unity

In a widely read book edited by R. J. Ballon, entitled *Doing Business in Japan*, Susumu Takamiya described Japanese business organizations as not mere mechanisms geared for work. He saw them as human groups in which the performance of an individual is recognized only as part of the performance of his total group.

THE UNIQUENESS OF JAPANESE MANAGEMENT

This same theme was described in a Harvard Business Review article by the late Howard Van Zandt entitled, "How to Negotiate in Japan." Harmony and unity were attributed to a Buddhist teaching called *shujō no on*, or a feeling of obligation to all living things and to the world for one's success. An employee who accepts this orientation attributes his success to other people's assistance and luck, not to his own intelligence and hard work.

Conversely, Americans are described as valuing individualism and independence as an overriding characteristic of their existence. For example, W. C. Ouchi, in his book *Theory Z*, described Americans as considering close relationships in the workplace unacceptable. That is to say, it is unhealthy to mix personal feelings with formal working relationships.

Paternalism

"Lifetime employment" is a household phrase attributed to Japanese, not American, personnel policies. The employee makes a total commitment to the company, and in return he receives a host of benefits which protect him on and off the job.

It has often been reported that Americans make a clear distinction between work and private life. The employee and employer clearly understand that the connection between them is limited to the activities directly related to the completion of a specific job.

Seniority

Japan's seniority system is strongly related to *nenkō*, or a seniority-order wage system. The new graduate steps on the wage escalator at age 22 and gets off at retirement age between 55 and 60. Since wages are paid primarily on the basis of age and length of service, the longer he stays with the firm the more he earns. This system is also perceived as creating unity and harmony since it provides for a safe, fair and undebatable progression of income throughout a career.

The American experience of "rags to riches" success, on the other hand, has resulted in a wage and reward system based primarily on performance. A Japanese proverb states, "A standing nail will be hammered down." The seniority system neatly reflects the Japanese attitude of wanting to "stand in," as opposed to the American respect for those who "stand out."

Objective of Comparative Study

While the above attributes assigned to Japanese and American societies and organizations may be generally true, when their application in firms within the pharmaceutical industry, for instance, is compared specifically, some myths emerge. Pharmaceutical companies engage in similar activities, from research and development to marketing. The industry, both in Japan and America, is considered innovative, information oriented, and "high-tech."

Method

In-house company magazines designed for internal reporting purposes, as opposed to publications for external audiences, were utilized in this comparative study. Employee publications and newsletters currently represent one of the most widely used communication programs by firms in both the U.S. and Japan. They are sent to virtually 100 percent of the employees, are published regularly, present material in detail and serve bottom-up, horizontal and top-down communication needs. They reflect management policies as well as employee needs and interests.

Company magazines of twenty-five U.S. and twenty-nine Japanese companies were eligible for this study after a rigorous selection process. Forty-two Japanese and thirty-four American companies were contacted in the original sample.

Articles on "group harmony" were defined as those articles in which the major thrust was to express and/or aim at at least one of the following concepts:

1. Cooperative work relationships among employees

THE UNIQUENESS OF JAPANESE MANAGEMENT

2. Mutual understanding among employees, and/or employees and management
3. Trust relationships among employees, and/or employees and management
4. Group morale
5. Group consensus
6. Smooth human relations in a company
7. Employees' participation in the company operations
8. A company's participation in various activities in order to create a sense of membership among employees, e.g., sports meetings, club activities, community activities and picnics.

Three sub-categories of group harmony were identified as regular, employees' participation, and entertainment.

The regular category included articles whose major thrust fell within the definition of group harmony. Examples of such articles are those on quality circles; a company's participation in various activities; awards to a company; a company's cooperation with a government campaign to prevent illness; a focus on one employee or group of employees and/or management by introducing their hobbies, interests, family, and other human interests; credit unions; and a company's services to employees. Articles about employees and/or executives were included because the intention of these articles is to add a touch of human appeal for the readers. This creates reader interest in others in the company, which serves to enhance group morale and a sense of unity. However, messages from management were not included so long as the major thrust of the article was business, as is explained below.

If an article was either submitted by an employee or an employees' family, that article went under "employees' participation in company magazines." Examples of such articles were essays, poems, opinions, pictures, photographs and paintings contributed by employees or their families.

Examples of "entertainment" articles are games, crossword puzzles, quizzes, stories, essays, cartoons, pictures and current topics. These articles might have been written by the editors, management or outside writers, or were excerpts from other newspapers and magazines.

JAPANESE MANAGEMENT—A MYTH?

If an article focused on one of the following concepts, it was included under "paternalism":

1. A corporate commitment to satisfy the social as well as economic needs of employees
2. Holistic concern for employees' well-being by a company
3. Mutual dependency between management and employees
4. Employees' longing for protection by the company
5. The company assuming retirement, health and safety needs of its employees
6. Insurance, savings plans and other fringe benefits provided by the company
7. A company's support to employees' activities, i.e., sports and clubs
8. Services provided by the company
9. An employees' family involvement in activities and services provided by the company.

Paternalism was assumed to extend not only to employees but also to their family members. Examples of paternalism articles included extracurricular activities assisted by the company such as travel, clubs, parties and events; facilities for employees such as cafeterias, day-care centers and gyms; training and education provided by the company; scholarships to employees and employees' families; useful and helpful information on health, safety, and nutrition; and announcements of retirees, new employees, weddings, births, birthdays and service anniversaries.

If an article focused on one or more of the following concepts, it was included under "seniority":

1. Respect for long-service employees
2. Attention to the length of service in the company. Examples of these articles are service anniversaries, retirees, announcements, retirees' life styles and retired workers' meetings.

One of the main purposes of publishing company magazines is to raise the employees' awareness and deepen their understanding of the company's business, policies and financial situation, thus increasing productivity and ultimately profits. Therefore, company magazines publish articles dealing directly with these purposes. Examples include policies and procedures, a president's message to employees, financial data, new technology employed by the company, business meetings, conferences, new products, and mergers. The primary interest of this study was to see how Japanese and American companies communicate with their employees through the medium of company magazines other than by "business-only" articles. Therefore, articles on the company's business were not counted except to the extent that they included employees' participation in the company operations/business, e.g., quality circles.

The research design utilized one independent variable and a variety of dependent variables. The independent variable was a country, i.e., the U.S. or Japan. The dependent variables reflected the amount or frequency of different types of content.

Results

One surprising result discovered early in the analysis was that 32.4 percent of U.S. company magazine space was devoted to articles about the company, its business performance and policies. Only 9.1 percent of Japanese company magazine space was utilized for the same purpose. Business reporting was not a specific category considered as a subject for comparison. However, it was evident the performance of the firm was reported in great detail by American companies. The reasons for this remain speculative, but it may reflect American management emphasis on clear-cut, objective results versus the "soft" aspects of corporate culture considered important by Japanese management.

TABLE 2
Total Space Allocated (%)

Category	U.S.	Japan
Business	32	9
Harmony	36	59
Paternalism	28	30
Seniority	4	2

TABLE 3
Mean Percentage of Area and Number
of Articles of Japanese and American Companies
(Magazines by Category)

Category	Area/ Total (%)		Number of Articles/ Total (%)	
	Japan	U.S.	Japan	U.S.
Group Harmony total	59.2	35.8*	50.5	38.2*
Regular Employees' participation	22.5	26.2	24.8	31.6
	27.3	3.0*	16.4	0.8*
Entertainment	9.4	6.7	9.5	5.8
Paternalism	29.7	27.8	38.2	32.2
Seniority	2.0	4.0	1.7	4.7*

* By the use of statistical methods of analysis, these numbers were considered significantly different from what could have appeared by chance.

Fiction: Japanese Companies Are More Paternalistic Than U.S. Firms

Standard notions of Japanese emphasis on paternalism as differing from the American practice were not supported by this study. Both Japanese and U.S. magazines devoted considerable space to this matter. Japanese and American managements are equally concerned with employee welfare. Benefits beyond salary are evident in examples taken from articles in both countries. There is a comparable sensitivity to the employees' need for compassion, fairness and support beyond the boundaries of the work place.

Fiction: Japanese Companies Emphasize Seniority More Than U.S. Firms

It was evident from this study that neither Japanese nor U.S. firms talk much about seniority, at least in company magazines. The study results suggest managers in both countries are equally concerned with retaining competent personnel for a long time.

THE UNIQUENESS OF JAPANESE MANAGEMENT

An impression, unsupported by the analysis, is that U.S. magazines more often highlighted the long-service employee. This may reflect the fact that in Japan long-service employees are not "news," but may also indicate a desire of U.S. firms to promote the virtue and value of long-term employment.

Fact: Employee Participation Is Emphasized More in Japanese Firms

U.S. firms, as seen through the window of company magazines, are as concerned as their Japanese counterparts with harmony, unity, paternalism and seniority. Other studies have suggested these characteristics were uniquely Japanese.

A closer look at the category Group Harmony showed that employee participation as a sub-group of harmony and unity accounted for a striking difference between Japanese and U.S. firms. Only 3 percent of U.S. company magazine area was allocated to employees' participation. The number of actual articles was also significantly different.

Conclusion

Only the notion of greater employee participation within Japanese firms as opposed to U.S. firms was supported by this study, possibly reflecting a change in U.S. cultural assumptions of individualism. E. C. Nevis, in the Sloan Management Review, said that there are two major emerging attitudes in American management.

1. A desire for close, more affiliative relationships at work as well as in other spheres of life, and
2. An appearance of intergroup cooperation to achieve superordinate goals in situations that typically would be left to competitive, adversary mechanisms.

A study of company magazines supports the view that U.S. companies have moved in the direction of what might be considered traditional Japanese values. It would also support the notion of Japanese managers moving in the direction of individualism, at least where seniority is concerned.

JAPANESE MANAGEMENT—A MYTH?

Although the overall implications of such a study need further confirmation, the results certainly indicate new thinking is required relative to competitive advantages of Japanese firms. In the pharmaceutical industry, Japanese managers are no more concerned with group harmony in general or with paternalism and seniority than their U.S. counterparts.

Only two features stand out as unique to Japanese firms. The first is a relatively minimal interest in communicating hard facts on the state of the business. Japanese managers devote much more attention to "soft" aspects of the working environment. These results support the viewpoint that an American pharmaceutical firm is not a place for the total commitment of employees, but a place to work. Personal interests and hobbies are to be left at the entrance. The office is for business only.

Secondly, the results suggest Japanese companies in this study encourage greater employee participation in the firm. Rather than expecting the employee to "punch in," do his work and then "punch out," the employee demonstrates his or her range of interests beyond the mere expression of work.

Employee participation strengthens harmony within the organization. This encourages more bottom-up communication in a firm where top-down communication is the norm, and may result in a competitive edge through focusing human resources on quality performance.

Finally, nine of the forty-two Japanese companies refused to submit examples of their company magazines. They considered them to be confidential documents that should not be given to outsiders. Not one of the thirty-four U.S. companies responded in this fashion. This difference in attitude may reflect the openness of U.S. society and the level of internationalization achieved by U.S. companies. Japanese pharmaceutical firms are basically confined to their home market and reflect an insular mentality.

My wife's paper was accepted by her thesis committee and she received an M.S. degree in 1984. Subsequently we have both wondered if the results would be different if in-house magazines of U.S. companies operating in Japan were reviewed, compared with those published by the same companies for their U.S. employees. The question is obvious, "Do they act in Japan like the Japanese?" Although the analysis is not completed (two

THE UNIQUENESS OF JAPANESE MANAGEMENT

babies have cut into research time), early indications suggest a positive answer to the question.

The findings in the original paper did confirm my own experience of working on both sides of the Pacific. Japanese managers do take a personal interest in the non-job related aspects of an employee. These hobbies and other interests are expected to be brought into the firm where all can see and share in the activity.

During the late 1970s, we developed an entirely new site in Japan for a manufacturing facility and a laboratory. In the center of the site was a separate building that housed a cafeteria and conference rooms. Additionally, this building had a significant amount of floor space set aside for employees to practice the tea ceremony, flower arranging and other activities. It was considered natural to provide these facilities for the exclusive use of employees.

Many Americans argue that true organizational participation means involvement in "hard" business issues. Therefore, as the study indicated, U.S. firms communicated about company results far more frequently than Japanese firms. On the other hand, they failed to take notice of employees' interests. Participation is a two-way street. Lack of interest in the employee as a whole person may be rewarded by employees' lack of interest in the company beyond the specific tasks they were assigned to complete.

Chapter 7

THE JAPANESE COMPETITOR — SAMURAI OR WIMP?

American pharmaceutical firms experience Japanese competition only in Japan. Results to date have not been comforting. Japanese products and companies dominate the market. Given a modest forecast of current trends, Japanese competitors are certain to appear in other major markets. One cannot assume the pharmaceutical market is "different" from other markets so successfully penetrated by Japanese firms. Their strengths and weaknesses are best studied in Japan before a major presence offshore is realized.

The pharmaceutical market in Japan has grown rapidly and is fiercely competitive. Four hundred forty-two companies market almost 14,000 products to approximately 180,000 physicians. They employ 187,940 people, of whom more than 40,000 are medical representatives. No single company dominates the market and the concentration ratio is low. The top ten companies have less than a cumulative 39 percent share of the market.

For the American firm, Japan is unique in at least one important aspect. It is the only major market in which it must deal with Japanese competitors. The results are not comforting. Japanese-origin products account for 60 percent of the market, a share that has not eroded for the past ten years. Japanese companies also dominate the market. Of the top twenty companies in 1987, sixteen were wholly-owned Japanese firms. Two

THE JAPANESE COMPETITOR

American firms and two European firms were on the list but not one was in the top ten.

In recent years, an increasingly innovative research capacity has produced a stream of products, many of which have been marketed worldwide. The cover of the 1986 annual report of Merck & Co., Inc., the largest U.S. pharmaceutical company, featured five major new products. Two of these products were licensed from Japanese companies. In other instances joint ventures have been established to develop and market products originating from Japanese research.

Most license agreements reserve exclusive rights for the Japanese company in Japan and "other Asian countries." Wholly-owned subsidiaries have been established in many countries, but primarily in those which are geographically and culturally close to Japan. The experience in these countries is instructive, but not considered strategically important in creating an internationally competitive position.

The net result of all these activities is a very minor presence outside Japan. There are now over fifty subsidiaries abroad but they are accounted for by less than ten companies. Exports account for less than 5 percent of total sales and an insignificant production base has been established outside Japan.

Nevertheless, the trend is definitely in one direction. Public and private statements by Japanese executives speak of the necessity to grow abroad, to increase the percentage of foreign sales, and to control development and marketing activities in Europe and the United States. It is therefore only a matter of time before Japanese competition becomes a fact of business life in countries outside Japan.

Given the experience of American firms in Japan, serious consideration should be given to the nature of Japanese competition. What are it's strengths and weaknesses? Is the dominance of Japanese competitors in Japan likely to be transferable outside of their home market? Answers to these questions and lessons learned in Japan are an important beginning in devising strategic responses to a new competitive challenge.

Competitive Options

In their book, *Kaisha, the Japanese Corporation,* Abegglen and Stalk listed four competitive fundamentals chosen by successful Japanese companies, i.e.:
1. A growth bias
2. A preoccupation with actions of competitors
3. The creation and ruthless exploitation of competitive advantage
4. The choice of corporate financial and personnel policies that are economically consistent with all of the preceding.

These same characteristics can be found in the pharmaceutical industry to varying degrees. However, two factors are unique to this industry. The approval of new drugs is regulated by the Ministry of Health and Welfare, and initial product prices and subsequent revisions are mandated by the National Health Insurance system. These two government-regulated processes do restrict the range of competitive options. For example, new products generally require eighteen months for approval after new drug applications are submitted to the ministry. Price listing may require another three to four months. Therefore, competitors are well aware of potential new products long before they actually enter the market.

Pricing in Japan, and for that matter in most parts of the world, is not what one would consider free market pricing. Neither can one consider this to be a mass market since the purchasing decision, or more accurately the prescribing decision, is in the hands of physicians, not the end user. Because drug dispensing in Japan does provide certain economic benefits, there is an element of price in the decision to select one drug over another. But the physician must consider the benefits and risks for individual patients in his selection of drug therapy, a decision independent of price. These factors set the pharmaceutical industry apart from automobiles and television sets.

One aspect of Japanese competitive advantage has become familiar to millions of consumers. It is product quality. Since the dawn of the modern drug era, quality has been a concern to drug manufacturers all over the world. The risk inherent in supplying even one contaminated vial, or one substandard tablet, to a patient is simply too high to be neglected. Japanese

THE JAPANESE COMPETITOR

firms will not find competitive advantage here. Surveys of Japanese drug quality do not indicate superiority over their Western counterparts.

The manufacturing capability of Japanese firms is also well known. Cost control measures, just-in-time inventory, and the scale of manufacturing have resulted in competitive advantages. There is some evidence that drug manufacturers in Japan have more fully automated their capacity to produce a variety of dosage forms. They have substantially reduced the number of employees in production. For example, U.S. firms have 36 percent of their employees in production compared with 29 percent in Japanese companies.

This relative advantage is not likely to have a serious impact on U.S. firms. This is not a production-driven industry. The history of new drug discovery indicates dosages are now measured in milligram quantities rather than grams, which further minimizes the need for production capacity. Products derived from advances in biotechnology also limit the need for huge biochemical plants. Processing a hepatitis vaccine from whole blood or insulin from animal organs requires a different level of capacity than the same products produced from yeast or bacteria.

Another aspect of Japanese corporate culture considered advantageous has been a focus on the long-term versus short-term. In the pharmaceutical business, it normally requires up to ten years for a product discovery to reach the market. This has forced management to make long-term commitments to investments in R&D and manufacturing. One cannot easily turn research projects on and off. There is no quick fix for a product with a suspicious side effect profile.

It is clear that various options employed so successfully by Japanese management in a range of industries are not available to Japanese pharmaceutical firms. In other instances, foreign competition has pre-empted the Japanese from competitive advantage. Standard wisdom dictates we must look elsewhere for reasons to explain the success of Japanese drug houses in their home market. This cannot be explained away by accusations of an "unlevel playing field." There are rational, explainable strengths utilized quite effectively by Japanese firms to counter multinational competition.

JAPANESE MANAGEMENT—A MYTH?

Competitive Strengths

R&D. Few Japanese-origin drugs have been recognized as "breakthrough" products. Many drugs widely sold in Japan are in fact not marketed abroad. R&D in Japan has been focused on a capacity to achieve small-step innovations. It provides not first generation, but second and third generation products that are improvements over the original model.

Case after case can be cited to prove this innovative capability. The scenario goes something like this. Japanese scour the world for new advances. They attend international medical meetings in droves. They constantly send study teams abroad. They pore over scientific literature translated from many languages. Each firm has well-organized licensing departments. Every new drug is scrutinized and an intense effort is made to bring it into their particular firm for development and marketing. More often than not, the originator does not have a capacity to develop the product in Japan or resources are concentrated on getting the product marketed in Europe and the U.S.

The successful Japanese company at this point learns a great deal about the merits of its licensed compound. It also determines its weaknesses. Research programs are initiated to find potential product candidates both free of patent conflicts and free of the limitations of the original breakthrough. Very often the process succeeds.

An example is the antibiotic market in Japan, the single largest therapeutic category, which is dominated today by cephalosporin products, originally discovered by the British National Research Council and developed by Glaxo in England and Eli Lilly in the United States. An Eli Lilly-origin product still holds the No. One position in the oral market but the injectable market is owned by Japanese competitors.

The point is that Japanese firms do not suffer from a "not invented here" syndrome. Their development staff is given resources and a status usually reserved for the basic research staff in foreign companies.

Developmental efforts also result in innovative new product forms. Typically, an American firm will concentrate on a limited number of formulations while their Japanese competitors offer several dosage forms, e.g., long-acting forms, granules, tablets, capsules, etc. A small advantage in the frequency of a daily dose or a unique product form can often be parlayed into a higher reimbursable price or other marketing advantages.

This competitive strength is a commitment to formulation development. While it is certainly not the stuff of major news articles, it does sell the product and mirrors the diversity of models and features so much a part of our daily life. A look into any store in Japan confirms the range of products available to the consumer. Japanese manufacturers pay attention to the needs of their customer.

Marketing. On the surface, the methods of selling pharmaceutical products in Japan seem similar to other markets. Medical representatives (detailmen) are responsible for the day-to-day contact with physicians. They report to district managers and the country is organized into regions, with a vice president of sales at the top. Sales training departments, market research, advertising agencies and office systems all exist here in one form or another.

Below the surface, it is another matter. Medical representatives all have a desk in an office to which they report at the beginning and the end of each day. Here they share information with their colleagues and review moves made by competitors. The intensity of contact with physicians and paramedical personnel is very high. Services are offered in great abundance. A relationship is established between the medical representative and his customers that goes far beyond providing product information. He is always there, always available, always ready to serve.

The same level of contact is made with wholesalers, who distribute virtually all ethical drugs to hospitals and clinics in Japan. The result is an intimate knowledge of market trends, prescribing habits and financial factors affecting the sale. Company representatives know their customers and fit the peculiar characteristics of their products to customer needs.

Personnel. Participation is the operative word as employees interweave their personal and business relationships so the two are indistinguishable. Success on the job is related to the success of the group. Financial rewards are made to the group and the most successful help their less talented colleagues to perform better.

JAPANESE MANAGEMENT—A MYTH?

These techniques for organizing and structuring the sales effort enhance morale and wrap each potential customer in a warm blanket of information and service. The net result is a loyal customer. Key investigators, professors, and the top management of important wholesalers are well known to the senior management of Japanese companies. They are not isolated from the customer, unaware of his needs.

Competitive Weaknesses

It is possible in the pharmaceutical industry that Japanese competitive power in Japan is a reflection of the relative weakness of competition from outside and a very favorable internal environment for growth. Management skills have not been challenged by adverse conditions. As it is a regulated industry, government actions have been supportive. Products, by means of licensing, have been available at a modest cost. Volume growth has been at double digit percentage rates for an uninterrupted span of time. Oil shocks, currency realignments and international political upheavals do not cause major dislocations in the pharmaceutical industry. Is the industry complacent and not up to the challenge of entering new, unfamiliar markets?

The management of Japanese pharmaceutical firms is in a transitional period. Family management is typical in many firms and at this time second-generation family members are running the businesses. A generalization can be made concerning the historical development of most major pharmaceutical companies in Japan. The founder, usually an entrepreneur in any business language, moved the firm from its roots as basically a wholesaler and/or a purveyor of tonics and herbal medicines to a research-oriented marketer of ethical drugs. His son(s) enjoyed a boom in the demand for health care and an expansion of the health insurance system during the 1960s and 1970s. It was virtually impossible not to annually increase sales and profits.

During the 1980s the environment has changed in many ways. Mandated price reductions have slowed growth. Product development costs have escalated. Products obtained through licensing-in programs are harder

THE JAPANESE COMPETITOR

to come by. In short, competitive factors have changed the business. It is far more complex today compared with when this generation of management assumed control.

Utilization of professional management in the pharmaceutical industry has lagged behind other Japanese internationally competitive industries. This is primarily a result of not moving competent people into senior management positions that threaten management succession to third-generation family members. How such top management moves are resolved in the foreseeable future may be a key to Japanese competitiveness.

Another weakness is the preoccupation of management with the domestic market. This is not surprising given the size of the Japanese market. Also, few people in Japanese firms have had work experience outside Japan. Contact with foreigners has been limited to a small number of employees in the export department or overseas division. The number of people familiar with a foreign language is similarly small. Simply stated, foreign experts are considered outsiders and rarely rise to key executive positions or to the level of board director.

Virtually all employees in Japanese pharmaceutical firms are Japanese and live in Japan. Liaison offices established outside Japan have been staffed with Japanese employees, and a foreigner employed by a Japanese firm is still an oddity, particularly in the U.S. or Europe. These "second-class citizens" enjoy no power in the inner councils of the company and are used mainly as interpreters for senior management.

R&D. As mentioned previously, the Japanese firm has mobilized a respectable innovative research capacity. All too often, however, the research function is similar to a castle, isolated from senior management by a moat of elitism and patronage to select members of the research establishment. Japanese firms have not yet integrated the total company effort required to register products worldwide.

One aspect of this problem is evident in the number of medical doctors employed by Japanese pharmaceutical firms. The number is very limited because of an inflexible compensation system that does not accommodate the needs of such professionals. Although this is not a disadvantage in Japan, it could prove to be very shortsighted outside Japan.

JAPANESE MANAGEMENT—A MYTH?

Personnel. New college graduates are surveyed annually in Japan to determine the type of industry and the specific company they would prefer to enter. Since the decision to enter a particular company is often a career commitment, the long-term viability of the company is an important aspect of the decision. Popular companies are considered to have a future. Pharmaceutical companies do not appear on these lists. This is not to say they do not get good people, but they are not getting the top students or the students from the best schools.

Given the people they do get, pharmaceutical firms are far behind other industrial firms in providing training at executive programs abroad. In any given year there are 15,000 Japanese attending schools in the U.S., but only an insignificant percentage are sponsored by pharmaceutical firms. Such personnel policies reflect the insular nature of management and the lack of a professional approach to management.

The Competitive Challenge

The general nature of the challenge has been stated by Abegglen and Stalk:

"In industry after industry, from steel to television to autos, the competitive thrust into world markets of the kaisha has followed a similar pattern: rapid growth of the Japanese market; fierce competition in Japan for market share; steadily improving cost and quality position of the leading Japanese companies; then an export drive by the domestic winners from 'Fortress Japan's' maturing industry, their base position protected from the lack of foreign competition in the Japanese market."

Much of the above is menacingly familiar to observers of the Japanese pharmaceutical industry. It is also clear that an appropriate competitive response is best learned in Japan, before advantages shift away from the American competitor. Will the Japanese market, second largest in the world, be forfeited to Japanese competitors?

None of the strengths that have propelled Japanese firms and products into a dominant position are surprising, unique or mysterious in business terms. The most appropriate strategic response is to match the Japanese strengths on their home ground.

THE JAPANESE COMPETITOR

American companies in Japan employ 10 percent of the total pharmaceutical work force. It is not surprising that this also approximates their "controlled" market share. With few exceptions, American companies have not matched their Japanese competitors in the intensity of market coverage. They have, by design or choice, remained aloof from the distribution channels, government officials, and key decision makers in medical circles.

One-fourth of the American companies with a presence in Japan do not have laboratories to conduct developmental studies. Two-thirds of the companies are not conducting basic research in Japan. Such statistics seem to indicate a relative lack of American company aggressiveness toward the market, as compared with the history of their involvement in other major markets.

Fortunately, one does sense a revitalization of moves to increase the potential power of American firms in Japan. A casual reading of the trade press over recent months highlights such moves as: new investments in laboratory facilities; an increase in the number of medical representatives; announcements of new or expanded production facilities; board of director meetings in Japan; listings on the Tokyo Stock Exchange; taking over distribution functions formerly performed by Japanese companies; scientific and research awards by foreign firms; capital increases and increased equity positions in established firms.

Weaknesses in Japanese firms do exist. Few managers of Japanese pharmaceutical firms are intimately familiar with the American market. As they move offshore they will need to deal with American employees, an experience unfamiliar to Japanese personnel managers. Business strategies employed in Japan may not be transferable elsewhere. Such weaknesses may be a window of opportunity for American competitors if aggressive moves are made to capitalize on them.

All too often American firms appear to be intimidated by Japanese competitors. Aggressive moves are not made to take advantage of weaknesses. Soon after joining Merck & Co., Inc. in 1976, I was impressed with the commitments of time, money, and people devoted to expanding the firms' presence in European markets. Managers felt they could take on large na-

JAPANESE MANAGEMENT—A MYTH?

tional companies and win market share. The behavior of Merck in Japan was completely different. Moves made in Japan were timid in comparison with those made in Europe. This type of behavior permits weak Japanese companies to survive, correct their problems, and become fierce competitors.

No one has said competing in Japan is easy, but neither should anyone believe that there are institutionalized barriers to success. Companies have learned they can match Japanese competitors in the fundamentals outlined at the beginning of this chapter. They have also proved that the rewards for a significant position in the Japanese market are high. The potential payback is enhanced by a consistent commitment to excel.

There are samurai-like competitors and wimp-like competitors in Japan's high-tech markets. They both benefit when American firms fail to recognize the difference and fail to take advantage of weak positions. The competitive front is not impregnable. Successful American firms analyze their competition as thoroughly as their customer. Wimps can be pushed aside. Even samurai competitors are not invincible because every company must use people to succeed. Some of the strengths and weakness of these people are described in the next chapter.

Chapter 8

JAPANESE COMPANY EMPLOYEES

> *Over 187,000 men and women are employed by Japan's pharmaceutical industry. They share characteristics common to employees in other high-tech firms: they are loyal, hard-working, generally dedicated to one-company careers, not trade unionized and oriented toward working within a group. Their educational backgrounds parallel those of pharmaceutical employees worldwide. They have aspirations for top management positions. Unique aspects set them apart from employees in other industries. Knowing your employee is as important as knowing your customer.*

For several years, Japanese employees have been analyzed by business and lay publications, motion pictures, seminars on competitiveness, and doctoral dissertations. They have been portrayed as both the villains and the heroes of Japan's economic achievements. Appearing to some as being one step removed from slaves, living in "rabbit hutches," subsisting on a diet of raw fish and rice and oppressed by management. To others they are seen as emancipated workers, dedicated to quality, protected from unfair, inhuman employment practices, and happy in their quality circles.

Japan's competitive advantage is ascribed to such employee characteristics as working hard, loyalty, intelligence, participativeness, honesty, and dedication. Managers from other countries observe in awe the Japanese

JAPANESE MANAGEMENT—A MYTH?

statistics on days lost due to strikes, rates of absenteeism, productivity increases, and service records.

However, as with any generalization or stereotype there is as much myth as reality in the image. The longer one works in Japan, the more difficult it is to generalize about the Japanese employee. "They" do not all look or dress alike. Some work hard, others goof off. Some are really smart, others are dumb. Some come to work on time, others are habitually late.

Generalizations are useful in evaluating the potential risks and rewards for an American company conducting business in Japan. Cultural factors must be considered when personnel policies are implemented in a Japanese subsidiary. Who are these employees? What are their strengths and weaknesses? How do they differ from employees in other Japanese industries? These and other questions are important for the multinational pharmaceutical firm for three reasons. First, motivating employees in Japan may be the most critical factor determining success or failure. Secondly, competitors in Japan are primarily Japanese companies and a competitive analysis must include the relative strengths of the people employed by these firms. Thirdly, recognizing changes in the expectations of employees may be a recruiting opportunity for alert firms.

Many assumptions regarding the Japanese work force are derived from studies of assembly line workers in industries like steel and automobiles. A high-tech industry like pharmaceuticals employs very few people who toil away at repetitive tasks. Therefore, it may be risky to assume the tired cliches are applicable in knowledge-intensive industries.

Characteristics of the Work Force

Men and women employed by the pharmaceutical industry in Japan represent a small proportion of the total work force. In 1987 there were 59,110,000 employed people in Japan. The pharmaceutical industry employed 187,940 people, or 0.3 percent of the total work force.

Pharmaceutical employees are not in the mainstream of employment patterns. If a new graduate of a high school or university enters the phar-

JAPANESE COMPANY EMPLOYEES

maceutical industry, he is unique among his classmates. In a group-oriented society, he is different from the very beginning of his career. At high school class reunions and family gatherings, he may be alone in his chosen profession.

It should be noted that Japanese employees do not consider their particular talents as being attached to the person, marketable to any company. A person's net worth is identifiable with a specific company, not with his profession. In a study conducted among children from Japan and the United States, most American children responded to the question "What does your father do?" with, "My father is a lawyer (or carpenter, or accountant)," while Japanese children responded by saying, "My father works for Sumitomo (Hitachi, Mitsui, etc.)."

When a Japanese employee refers to his company he uses the word *uchi*, which also means "home." For example, "In my home we manufacture antibiotics." This is a very personal reference compared with the usual third-party reference made in the U.S.

This may be one reason why the trade union movement in Japan is limited. A driver or a carpenter in one company does not feel a sense of "brotherhood" with drivers or carpenters from other companies. His sense of loyalty is to other employees in his own house or company. Unions exist on a national scale but high-tech employees are largely untouched by their activities, campaigns and slogans.

Products sold by the pharmaceutical industry are promoted directly to physicians. They are not publicized in the mass media and therefore attract little attention from the general public. Company identification is socially important in a vertical society such as Japan, where rank and position determine the nature of so many responses. For example, a suitable marriage partner is often "arranged" for a young man or woman. The opportunities are greater, and the image more positive, if the potential partner works in Sumitomo Bank rather than XYZ Pharmaceutical Company.

Because of the above factors, an employee in the pharmaceutical industry is by definition different from other employees in Japanese industry. One is reluctantly, but objectively, led to conclude that the brightest and best Japanese young people are not lining up to enter pharmaceutical companies.

JAPANESE MANAGEMENT—A MYTH?

This may have important consequences when we consider the relative competitive power of these firms.

If the labor pool of prospective employees is relatively small, the number of companies competing for them is not. In 1985, there were 1,369 pharmaceutical companies in Japan, a number which has been very stable for the past ten years. Some 32 percent of these companies are ethical drug companies, while 45 percent are over-the-counter (OTC) drug companies, and the remaining companies sell both ethical pharmaceuticals and OTC products.

One surprising statistic is that 73 percent of the 1,369 companies have only 100 employees or less. Only 2.8 percent of the companies have more than 3,000 employees, demonstrating that the pharmaceutical work force is organized into relatively small companies. Many of the well-known characteristics of Japanese employees are those found in large organizations. In fact, most if not all of the studies on employees have been conducted in large companies.

Employment conditions in large enterprises are quite different from those in small companies, particularly in providing opportunities for training, overseas experience, lateral transfers, and overall development of a person's capabilities.

A significant proportion of the pharmaceutical work force is employed by family-managed companies. Well over half of the major Japanese pharmaceutical companies are currently managed by second or third-generation family members. This is not to imply that family management is by definition bad, of course. But one can assume that "professionally" managed firms have different philosophies, particularly as they relate to personnel policies. One would expect less nepotism, more emphasis on merit versus seniority, and a systems-oriented approach to training and development.

To summarize, pharmaceutical companies in Japan:
1. Employ a very small percentage of the total labor force.
2. Are organized into relatively small units.
3. Are not well known to the general public.
4. Are primarily family managed.
5. Compete for a relatively small pool of talent.

6. Do not get the brightest and best output of the educational system.
7. Are largely untouched by national union activities.

Table 4 sums up the organization of employees within the pharmaceutical industry. The data indicate that as recently as 10 years ago employees in the production area of pharmaceutical companies were the dominant employee group. Their relative number has decreased as firms have increased production requirements through automation and productivity improvements. Most employees in production have a high school education and a significant number are females.

TABLE 4
Employees in the Japanese Pharmaceutical Industry (%)

Year	Total	Administration	Production & Engineering	R&D	Marketing/Sales
1975	135,759	19,863 (14.6)	58,425 (43.0)	17,480 (12.9)	39,991 (29.5)
1980	155,415	20,955 (13.5)	62,420 (40.2)	21,952 (14.1)	50,088 (32.2)
1985	187,940	30,009 (16.0)	65,028 (34.6)	28,888 (15.4)	64,015 (34.1)

The relative number of employees in administration has also declined. Specific data are not available to indicate the functional breakdown of this section, but experience would suggest that the number of employees has increased in the area of computer-information systems and decreased in other staff functions.

On the other hand, total employment has increased primarily because of expansion in the R&D and marketing functions. These employees typically have university degrees and are male. Compared with those for production employees, salary scales and other benefit programs must be more flexible. Production-driven personnel policies are often inadequate for these professionals.

It is rare to find females in management positions. In fact, outside the R&D area very few female college graduates are recruited into pharmaceutical companies. Furthermore, it is generally expected that a woman will leave the company when she marries, so training programs for them are minimal. This potential pool of talent is underutilized but there is not much change taking place.

There are now 15.84 million working women, or 40 percent of Japan's total work force. However, they still hold relatively few managerial positions. A recent study by Jane Condon, author of *A Half Step Behind*, indicated only 6.4 percent of scientists, 2.4 percent of engineers, and 6.2 percent of managers in Japan were women. These percentages are probably lower in the pharmaceutical industry, particularly in management.

Benefit programs for pharmaceutical employees do not differ significantly from those offered in other high-tech firms. In recent years, the retirement age has been increasing from 55 to 57. Board of director-level employees are often exempt from this retirement rule, serving at the discretion of the president. Recently, however, more companies have implemented retirement rules for such employees.

Employee Strengths and Weaknesses

The pattern of employment in the pharmaceutical industry does prompt several, albeit speculative, conclusions concerning the quality of employees. Differences between entry-level employees in Japan are narrower than in other countries because of the homogeneous, highly educated nature of the population and a similarity in cultural and family factors. Personnel managers in Japan do not need to deal with racial differences, regional disparities of education and training or ethnic differences of behavior.

However, differences in corporate cultures exist. Over time, employees' attitudes and skills develop differently, and the pharmaceutical industry is no exception.

Japanese pharmaceutical companies have a very small presence outside Japan. Foreign sales account for less than 5 percent of total sales. Very few companies have foreign subsidiaries and less than 4 percent of Japanese employees have lived and worked in a foreign country.

The result is a lack of familiarity with foreign languages, management practices and systems. There are an insignificant number of foreign employees working for Japanese pharmaceutical firms. The net impact is an insular mentality and a lack of outside stimuli challenging purely Japanese solutions to problems.

Family management also puts a damper on risk-taking or aggressive actions. Employees learn not to "rock the boat" and tend to become more bureaucratic as they advance in age. Since top management positions are more limited, employees learn to court favor from the chosen few by following rather than leading.

It is not surprising, therefore, that very few pharmaceutical executives have equaled the status of business leaders from other industries, nor do they serve on respected councils of key business associations. They are generally unknown outside their company or the pharmaceutical trade organizations. Few are called upon to speak at international conferences or participate in international business seminars.

Positive comments can be made about employees engaged in production and formulation development. Japanese pharmaceutical companies have led the world in automating various medicinal processes. Quality levels are high and the number of operators and inspectors is low. Many of the pharmaceutical factories in Japan are state-of-the-art facilities. GMP (Good Manufacturing Practice) standards are adhered to, improved upon, and widely in place. Employees are challenged to improve productivity without compromising quality. Enthusiasm runs high, turnover is low, factories are spanking, "squeaky" clean, computerized and efficient.

The R&D environment is less positive. Pharmaceutical firms have not attracted the most qualified scientists, who consider industry research positions as having less status than academia. Scientists are generally isolated within the firm in an organizational cocoon. Secrecy is considered more important than the intellectual stimulation achieved through interactions with outside researchers. Japanese scientists do attend international meetings in large numbers, but their colleagues are almost 100 percent Japanese and research is conducted almost exclusively in Japan.

A mixed positive/negative picture exists in the area of marketing. The standard pattern has been to sell and serve with humility. Training programs stress the need to establish relationships and bow deeply to doctors. Creative marketing personnel are stifled and such programs reduce many employees to mere order-takers. On the other hand, there are emerging patterns of enlightened training in product knowledge as opposed to in-depth knowledge of the price list. Physicians are demanding more than a personable representative with money to pay for golf games and departmental social gatherings.

Such changes challenge sales managers to seek potential salesmen with different qualities not recruited for in the past. Training programs will be altered and the role of the representative will become more sophisticated. Working "hard" or working long hours at mindless paper tasks will give way to working "smart" and increasing the level of product knowledge and the benefit/risk aspects of drug therapy.

Overall, employees in the pharmaceutical industry have not been challenged by economic adversity. Skills have not been sharpened to deal with severe threats to profitability or bottom-line viability. The industry has been buffered from recession, currency adjustments and political instability. In one sense, the Japanese national health reimbursement system has been an umbrella under which companies could not only survive, but prosper without extraordinary levels of intelligence or effort. The company's existence appeared secure. There are few cases of bankruptcy or the need to relocate and retire substantial numbers of employees.

Factors such as these have not honed employees' competitive skills. Neither do they create conditions that attract employees motivated by an international competitive challenge, or who desire to achieve highly visible top-level positions. However, certain companies are proving that this type of employee can be recruited by enlightened, professional management. They are demonstrating that new skills can be learned, product knowledge does pay off, and research innovation earns international respect.

The Bottom Line

Japanese pharmaceutical companies are a dominant force in their home market, have grown steadily, discovered products of international importance, and have prospered. Such success did not happen automatically or without the efforts of a dedicated work force. Employees, not factories, make a company.

Advances have been made from the past when pharmaceutical companies were mere wholesalers or traders. They are facing challenges never encountered during uninterrupted periods of growth and prosperity. Internationalization is not just a slogan, it is a prerequisite for continued growth. Such changing patterns impose difficulties unexperienced by the previous generation of managers and will have both positive and negative effects on employee behavior.

American firms operating successfully in Japan have demonstrated that their Japanese work force is capable of performing at a level of excellence comparable with employees in any other country. They have proved it is possible to attract a quality person who learns quickly and responds positively to programs that enhance his value as a productive, motivated employee.

Narrow-minded, insular, family-oriented personnel policies are no longer an appropriate response for young people eager to maximize their potential contributions to the firm. Aspirations for high-level positions cannot be denied. As in other industries, managers must learn to attract the best talent and motivate it with flexible, professional personnel policies.

Japan is a fertile ground for the development of an internationally competitive high-tech industry. Realizing this objective requires the best possible employees. Some companies will find them, manage them wisely, and develop them with challenging programs. The employees in these companies will demand the best and become the best.

Employees, particularly those in high-tech firms, are demanding more of their employers than ever before. Many of the old stereotypes are no longer useful guides to personnel management in Japan. Staying on top of these changes can open up many competitive advantages for American firms. Many Japanese personnel departments are mired in the past or locked into policies that no longer attract or retain key employees of all ages. One stereotype, lifetime employment, is notably out of date. What this can mean for the alert American firm is explored in the next chapter.

Chapter 9

HALF-A-LIFETIME EMPLOYMENT

> *The demographics of Japan's population are changing rapidly as the birth rate drops and everyone lives longer. Life expectancy is now the longest in the world. The society is aging. Company pyramids are bulging at the top. Moving up the escalator is no longer an automatic process, therefore motivating experienced employees is a new challenge for management. Dissatisfaction at all levels is creating a unique of opportunity for American firms to attract and retain excellent people.*

Life expectancy for Japanese males is now 75 years at birth. University graduates generally enter the work force at age 22 and retire at age 57. They have a working life of 35 years (22—57) and a non-working life of 40 years (75—57+22). So-called lifetime employment should more appropriately be called half-a-lifetime employment. Lifetime employment is a myth for most Japanese workers. Other such myths exist.

The caliber of personnel management in Japan has been overrated for a long time. Visitors marvel at the discipline and motivation of the work force. They speak eloquently about bottom-up decision making, quality circles, company songs and exercise routines performed each morning. They admire the dedication and loyalty of employees.

Japanese managers love to tell their American partners how they, and

HALF-A-LIFETIME EMPLOYMENT

only they, know the secrets of hiring good people, training them and creating a special sense of harmony among them. They insist Americans will never succeed in Japan because they cannot hire qualified people. From the time a visiting businessman steps off the airplane, and before he gets to the hotel, he is given at least one lecture on personnel practices in Japan. The most obnoxious ones are punctuated by the phrase, "we Japanese," as if the speaker was qualified to speak for the entire race.

In reality, a manager in Japan can be almost incompetent yet do a reasonable personnel job. This does not stop personnel managers from patting themselves on the back, but they have not yet faced many of the demographic challenges of a Western workplace, many of which are beginning to be true in Japan. Only a few factors need to be cited in defense of this statement.

Potential employees are easy to contact, given the short distances, clustering of universities, and one time per year entry of new employees. All speak the same language, read the same newspapers, and watch the same television programs. All share the same cultural heritage and went through the same educational process. Regional differences are minimal. Positive values and rules are well understood. Drug abuse is not a national problem. Entry-level wages do not vary significantly by educational training or among companies in the same industry.

Nevertheless, screening procedures are extraordinary, running the gamut from written examinations, interviews and reference checks, to private investigations. The latter are conducted in great detail. The practice would be considered an invasion of privacy in many countries. People who do not pass this most intimate scrutiny of their public and personal lives are quietly dropped from the list of "qualified" candidates.

It is not surprising that new employees are prepared to accept whatever management doles out. In fact, few Japanese at the age of 21 have been educated to express their own opinions, and those with this talent were probably weeded out in the first interview. Company trainers begin where professors left off, communicating what should be done and what should not be done in a one-way direction.

Sales training in the pharmaceutical industry is a good example. It is a

JAPANESE MANAGEMENT—A MYTH?

common practice in the U.S. to conduct role-playing exercises for both new and experienced representatives. One person is identified as the "doctor" and he is detailed by the representative on a product. Some companies in the U.S. will hire, on a part-time basis, residents and interns to take doctor roles. This practice sets up a risk-free environment in which the trainee can practice various approaches to deal with typical objections voiced by physicians in the real world. Basically, it is a two-way learning process.

In Japan the process of learning is quite different. It goes something like this: "I am the trainer and here is what you should tell the doctor about our products." The first time a representative gets an objection from a real-life doctor he has no idea what to say.

Salary administration in a Japanese company is equally uninspiring. Until the age of 30, everyone is basically on the same salary curve, a straight line in an upward direction. During the next ten years, there may be three salary levels, all parallel, but distinguishing between those on a fast track, the average performers, and the laggards. Between the ages of 40 and 50, the wheat gets separated from the chaff. Star performers achieve *buchō* (director) class, laggards are made *kachō* (manager), and the losers are given social titles but no real power. After the age of 50, three possibilities unfold. At the top is a seat on the board of directors; in the middle, a steady progression of salary increases, then out at age 57; at the bottom, a tapering off of salary increases and out as soon as possible.

Just as many Japanese managers have congratulated themselves on being "geniuses" in personnel administration, several factors have disturbed the classic pattern. Changing attitudes within three age groups are worthy of consideration. The entry-level employee, age 22; the mid-career employee, age 30-40; and senior employees, age 45-55. Each group is breaking the standard mold and causing consternation within the system.

The Entry-Level Employee

Recently, a Saturday night television quiz program questioned a panel on what was in and out of fashion. Surprisingly, universities were among the categories, and that venerable institution, Tokyo University, was considered out of fashion. This may have more significance than mere entertainment value. Young people, in growing numbers, want more than just a good image from their education.

More often than not, they have traveled abroad and gained exposure to situations in which they feel their talents could be recognized and rewarded accordingly. They are impatient with personnel systems that do not provide opportunities for individual effort. The typical "escalator" approach to salary administration is not an attractive option for many university graduates, particularly those with degrees in high-technology disciplines.

I have reviewed salary data obtained from 18 top pharmaceutical companies. The average monthly starting salary for a university graduate in 1987 was ¥160,196. The highest salary was ¥165,900 and the lowest ¥155,000, not much difference among a wide range of companies. Typically, the initial salaries for graduates of liberal arts courses were the same as for graduates with a scientific or technical degree.

Companies do not compete for entry-level talent by salary differentials. A prospective employee must decide which company to work for based upon other factors. As a result, foreign companies do not need to "buy" their way into the system. As long as the starting wage is competitive, they may focus on aspects of employment which are attractive to young people. The key is to be tuned into changing values and expectations.

I am not competent to evaluate the sociological factors that differentiate a 22-year-old Japanese male in 1989 compared with one in 1967. However, businessmen who interview entry-level employees will tell you few are shy about asking penetrating questions about company policies. One question in particular is frequently asked of American firms, "Who controls policy, the home office 8,000 miles away, or local managers?"

It is a myth that American firms cannot hire good people in Japan. Certain well-known examples of irresponsible behavior have perpetuated this idea but astute companies know it is not true. The key issue today is not the nationality of the firm, it is the management inside the firm. Both good and bad news about management travels fast in Japan. A good reputation must be nurtured carefully and protected with a great deal of vigor. The entering class of freshman employees is far more important to the future of a company than current earnings or current products.

The Mid-Career Employee

In 1987, 13.5 percent of the male population was between 30 to 40 years old. All of these men were born after World War II and were going to school when their fathers were rebuilding Japan. They did not experience poverty or hunger and they become more affluent every year. They are the "average" employees in most companies.

For example, in the sample of 18 companies cited earlier, the average number of male employees was 2,933. The average age of these employees was 37.4 with an average length of service of 14.6 years. Therefore, the average employee joined the firm at age 22.8, not surprising since very few people left these companies and everyone came in at an entry-level age. Other data indicate 95 percent of employees joining pharmaceutical firms stayed in the same firm for their entire career.

Salary data obtained in my survey are mentioned here only as an order-of-magnitude number. More accurate data are available from other sources and should be constantly updated. However, it was of interest to note that the spread of starting salaries among companies was within a 7 percent range, yet overall average salaries varied by as much as 46 percent. In other words, at the starting gate, money did not separate one company from another, but fifteen years later average salaries varied significantly. It is no wonder young applicants are asking serious questions of the employer before getting on board.

In short, the average male employee in my sample of firms was 37 years old, he worked for the same company for fifteen years, now earns a base monthly salary of $2,700 (¥125 = 1), and will be working in the company for another twenty years.

In the same survey, the average female employee was 29 years old and worked in the same company for nine years. Compared with male employees, females are seriously disadvantaged in terms of salary. There is at least a 10 percent salary differential, even when adjusting the data to account for length of service. Also, within the sample there are wide differences in the average salaries of females between companies as well as the average years of service. Some companies manage to get females out the door very quickly.

Thirty-year-old male employees are still mobile in terms of family responsibilities. Often, they want to take advantage of this opportunity to study at a school in the U.S. and obtain an MBA or advanced technical degree. In the past, a typical pattern was for the company to pick up the bill, in return for which the employee pledged his life to the firm. Today, many young people are financing a graduate education out of their own pockets, since they know they can use the degree for a higher-paying job with another firm after graduation. In other words, they get a nice return on their investment (ROI). Recruiting such individuals in the U.S. is an opportunity pursued by many American firms. In my own experience, we had the target of recruiting one MBA graduate a year. That goal was met easily. We often had several excellent candidates, and as time progressed we were receiving many unsolicited applications. A deliberate program to search out these people can provide a cadre of talented middle managers in a relatively short time.

At the upper end of the 30 to 40 age group are people electing a second career or dropping out of the system entirely. The obstetric wards of Honolulu hospitals are doing a brisk business with Japanese wives who elect to give birth on U.S. soil so that the child is a U.S. citizen. Other stories circulate about people who sell their real estate in Japan at a sizable profit and move to Australia where they can buy a larger home and invest the difference.

Such people undoubtedly represent a minuscule portion of the population. Nevertheless, the fact that they exist at all is indicative of changing value systems and attitudes. If a person is not challenged after fifteen years on the job and is looking at another twenty years of the same routine, he begins to think of other options. Such people are not necessarily failures and could do well in another company which offers a new challenge. Repotting can revitalize both plants and humans.

JAPANESE MANAGEMENT—A MYTH?

Fifteen years ago, few American companies were aggressively hiring new college graduates. Now they are actively recruiting, but have a gap in middle management talent. Outside recruiting is the only answer. Opportunities exist to fill these positions without upsetting internal morale.

The Senior Employee

Men between the ages of 45 and 55 should be in, or ready to move into, senior management positions. Many firms have the problem of supply exceeding demand. For twenty-four to thirty-four years these men have moved up the escalator only to find there is not enough room on the top floor to accommodate all those qualified. It is distressing and socially humiliating.

Companies have responded to this dilemma in a variety of ways. One is to create a new subsidiary, say a distribution company, and transfer surplus executives into new positions. Another response is to give these employees social titles which save face outside the company while changing nothing inside.

A more drastic response is an active, visible, out-placement service, which markets employees to other companies. Although this was unheard of in the recent past, there is no question that an American company can benefit from the situation. It can be a win/win game for both sides.

American companies in Japan award few tie pins for twenty-five years of service. Without a cadre of seasoned veterans at the top, the organization is unstable. Older employees help to guide younger people, act as a bridge to the future, and help American executives avoid the obvious pitfalls in implementing personnel policies. This does not mean American managers should jump at the first candidate with white hair. He may have been sitting by a window in a Japanese company for so long there is no spirit left in an otherwise healthy body.

Today, opportunities exist to screen and select enthusiastic senior men with the inner motivation to accept new challenges and prove their worth to former colleagues and friends. It has been my own personal pleasure to welcome many such people into an organization where they served with devotion and loyalty, making contributions beyond the ability of younger men.

A significant advantage of senior men is the network of contacts they have established during their careers. The Japanese practically invented the "old boy" network and it takes experience to work it properly. The fact that such people are more readily available today is an opportunity which should not be missed by American firms.

Beyond the Myths

In 1987, there were 34 million males between the ages of 20 and 59. Twenty-seven percent were between the ages of 30 and 40. Twenty-four percent were 45 to 54. Graphically, the population no longer looks like a pyramid, it more closely resembles a column. Company organizational structures, however, are like pyramids. Therefore lifetime employment can be translated as follows: "During my working life I will be working for one firm, but there may not be room for me at the top." As Table 5 indicates, however, even this description is suspect, since staying with one firm is only typical of employees in companies with 1,000 or more employees. Of all the companies in Japan, only 0.2 percent have more than 1,000 employees.

Loyalty to one firm is considered a virtue and a victory of Japanese personnel management policies. Seniority-based systems, or escalator-type movement up the salary and position ladder, worked well in the past when population demographics were different. Now they are a headache for per-

TABLE 5
Lifetime Employment — All Industries

No. of Employees	Percentage (1984)
1000 or more	85.5%
100 - 999	70.3
100 or less	53.9

JAPANESE MANAGEMENT—A MYTH?

sonnel managers. There are simply not enough positions on the top tier to satisfy the large percentage of working men in the 45 to 54 age group.

These dramatic changes have made it possible for American companies to secure a more age-balanced work force. Across the age spectrum there are new recruiting opportunities which were previously unheard of in Japan.

Changing attitudes among females also pose problems for the classic Japanese personnel management style. Much to the consternation of managers, women are not leaving the work force after the wedding ceremony. As was pointed out earlier, the average age of women in our pharmaceutical company sample was 29, about three years beyond the average age for marriage. This pattern implies a need to train women for responsibilities beyond serving tea and welcoming guests. To compound the problem, it is only a matter of time before women will want to get back into the work force after raising their children.

Young professionals are not content to wait 15 years before they can assume responsible positions. Carrying the bags of their seniors might be acceptable for men in their early 20s, but this dubious honor wears thin at age 35. The escalator appears dull, and a growing number of young people are refusing to step on board.

By many measurements the Japanese personnel system functions well for blue-collar workers. However, high-technology companies are not production-driven. As mentioned in an earlier chapter, ten years ago well over 40 percent of pharmaceutical company employees were in manufacturing. This number is now under 35 percent because a growing number of employees are in research and marketing positions.

Recently, a respected Japanese CEO, when talking about management of R&D activities, stated, "The research project team should have a large percentage of people under 40 years old." But he did not mention what should be done with 45-year-old researchers.

In many respects, these "problems" would be welcome in other countries. But in Japan they are serious and demand attention by managers accustomed to simpler solutions. Putting everyone on an escalator did not require great intellectual ability. It was simply a matter of efficiently monitoring the flow and making sure the "right" people got on at the

HALF-A-LIFETIME EMPLOYMENT

ground level. Now, more diversity is required in all aspects of personnel management, from salary scales to outplacement programs.

Successful American companies view these problems as opportunities. Also, enlightened Japanese managers are no longer giving lectures on paternalism and harmony, they are too busy changing their personnel systems to cope with new expectations and different social values. Old-fashioned managers are walking about in a daze, complaining about impatient youth, frivolous young women, and undedicated workers. They want women to retire after marriage, and men to retire at 57, hopefully sooner. However, many do not have a mandated retirement age for their own board of directors.

These management differences among companies are recognized by employees of all ages who desire more than the security, stability, and often dull routine of life on the escalator. American companies have never had a better chance to offer a rewarding alternative.

Chapter 10

THE JAPANESE HEALTH INSURANCE SYSTEM

> *By many measurements the Japanese are now the healthiest people in the world. An insurance system provides equality of health care throughout the land. Two types of insurance provide coverage for virtually everyone. A rapidly aging population is now imposing financial and management pressures on the system. Fundamental reform measures and innovative new directions will be implemented. Whether they work is a matter of great importance to the Japanese and the health care industry worldwide.*

The social insurance system in Japan is a remarkable achievement in providing universal equality of health care. Virtually every Japanese has access to health care and is covered by some form of insurance. Since its inception in 1922, the system followed the theme, "Medical Insurance for the Whole Nation."

At first, coverage was limited to factory workers. In 1938, a health insurance scheme was established for people engaged in agriculture, forestry and fishing. In the same year the Ministry of Health and Welfare made its debut. In 1959, a new National Health Insurance Act placed the entire nation under coverage. Since then, various modifications and amendments have been made to the system, particularly in 1983 when an Act of Health and Medical Services for the Aged was enacted. In 1984, insured persons were required to bear a portion of medical fees according to a fixed schedule. The fundamental structure and philosophy of the system has, however, remained intact.

To a significant degree, this system of health insurance has contributed toward achieving a high level of health care. By many measurements the Japanese can be considered the most healthy people in the world. Three examples are indicative of the trends. The first is an overall measurement of life expectancy (Table 6).

TABLE 6
Expectation of Life at Birth

	1947	1956	1966	1976	1987
Male	50.1	63.6	68.4	72.2	75.6
Female	54.0	67.5	73.6	77.4	81.4

The second is a dramatic improvement in infant mortality and neonatal deaths, both of which have rapidly declined, historically as well as in recent years (Table 7).

TABLE 7

Year	Infant Mortality	Neonatal Deaths
	(Per 1,000 Births)	
1940	90.9	38.7
1960	30.7	17.0
1980	7.5	4.9
1985	5.5	3.4

The third example shows data related to mortality in a wide variety of diseases. One normally is accustomed to looking at mortality rates as they appear in Table 8, published by the Ministry of Health and Welfare. Overall, mortality rates have decreased in the last twenty years. However,

TABLE 8
Changes of Mortality Rate by Cause
(Number of Persons per 100,000)

	1965	1975	1985
Malignant Neoplasm	108.4	122.6	156.1
Heart Diseases	77.0	89.2	117.3
Cerebrovasular Diseases	175.8	156.7	112.2
Pneumonia/Bronchitis	37.3	33.7	42.7
Accidents	40.9	30.3	24.6
Senility	50.0	26.9	23.1
Suicide	14.7	18.0	19.4
Diseases of Liver	10.0	13.6	14.3
Others	198.6	140.2	115.8
Total	712.7	631.2	625.5

TABLE 9
Change of Mortality Rate by Cause Adjusted by Age
(Number of Persons per 100,000)

	1965	1975	1985
Malignant Neoplasm	87.6	82.6	80.7
Heart Diseases	58.7	53.6	50.1
Cerebrovascular Diseases	133.5	92.7	46.6
Pneumonia/Bronchitis	34.8	21.6	16.8
Accidents	39.4	27.0	19.3
Senility	34.0	13.4	6.9
Suicide	12.3	13.8	13.2
Diseases of Liver	8.0	9.3	7.9
Others	214.9	117.2	71.7
Total	589.2	417.8	306.3

THE JAPANESE HEALTH INSURANCE SYSTEM

malignant neoplasms and deaths due to heart diseases have increased rapidly.

The Boston Consulting Group in Japan took the above statistics and adjusted them by age. That is, age was kept constant, and the result is shown in Table 9. By this measurement, the Japanese have become more and more healthy since 1965. This is a surprising view of the health of the Japanese people not normally considered by observers of Japan's health care system. The data indicate that for any given age group mortality rates have been decreasing over the past twenty years for a wide variety of diseases.

Types of Medical Insurance

As of March 31, 1986, 120,423,000 Japanese, virtually the entire population, were covered by two types of medical insurance. The first type is for those classified as employees. They and their dependents make up two-thirds of the total covered population. There are four subgroups in this type of insurance:
1. National government-managed health insurance for small enterprises (at least five employees).
2. Society (union)-managed health insurance for large enterprises (with more than 500 employees).
3. Seaman's Insurance for seamen.
4. Mutual Aid Associations for national and local public servants, public corporation employees and employees of private schools.

The second type covers 45,294,000 people classified as non-employees. It is divided into two subgroups:
1. Local government-managed National Health Insurance, and
2. Associations of persons engaged in the same occupation.

Benefits. The first type of insurance covers 90 percent of all medical fees for employees. For their dependents, 80 percent of hospital care and 70 percent of clinical care is covered. For non-employees in the second type of insurance, 70 percent of all medical fees are covered.

In each case above there is a cap on the patient's share of medical expenses. If the amount exceeds 54,000 yen per month, the excess is reim-

bursed. Other benefits, in addition to those described, are available to all insured persons. They include:
1. Allowances for loss of income due to temporary incapacitation because of sickness, injury or pregnancy.
2. Lump-sum payments for childbirth, nursing and funerals.
3. "Extraordinary" medical fees.

Financing. Given the comprehensive nature of insurance coverage, it is not surprising that medical care expenditures have grown at a compound annual rate of 15 percent since 1955. In 1985, they represented 5.0 percent of Japan's GNP or 132,300 yen per person.

Insurance programs for employees are financially sound, particularly since 1984 when the insured was required to bear a portion of medical fees. These programs benefit from the fact that relatively fewer aged people are enrolled. For example, the union-managed health insurance for large enterprises includes 24 percent of the total population, but only 10 percent of the over-65 age group.

Non-employee National Health Insurance is not financially sound. In 1985 government subsidies were required to cover 64 percent of the total costs. These programs enroll 38 percent of the total population but cover 64 percent of the over-65 age group.

Two major financial problems are now evident. First is the unbalanced financial health of the two types of insurance programs. Secondly, although the aged population represents 10 percent of the population it now accounts for almost 30 percent of all medical care insurance funds. This is becoming both an economic and political problem.

Table 10 documents revenue sources for Japan's national medical expenditures since 1960. As a percent of total revenue, out-of-pocket expenditures have declined while the relative share of government expenditures has increased. The Japanese government has recently attempted to limit the growth of medical expenditures to a rate that would not exceed the growth in national income. If medical expenses do grow at a faster rate, two policy choices are possible. First is to cut overall costs. Second is to increase the amount of revenue received from out-of-pocket sources. Both approaches are being pursued at the present time.

TABLE 10
National Medical Expenditures by Source of Revenue

Billion Yen (Percent)

	Individual		Employer		Government	
	Total	Out-of-Pocket	Paid-in Contribution	Paid-in Contribution	National Gov't	Municipal + Others
1960	410	123	105	101	64	15
	(100)	(30)	(26)	(25)	(16)	(3)
1970	2,496	482	685	640	603	86
	(100)	(19)	(27)	(26)	(24)	(4)
1980	11,981	1,322	3,493	2,897	3,646	641
	(100)	(11)	(29)	(24)	(30)	(6)
1985	16,016	1,919	8,704		4,347	1,046
	(100)	(12)	(54)		(27)	(7)
GAGR (%) '60-'85	16	12	16		18	18

Source: MHW

Providers. Health care personnel and facilities must be registered as providers of medical care benefits in order to submit bills for medical care. As of April 1, 1986 there were:

131,477	Medical Care Facilities
30,389	Pharmacies
219,623	Doctors
75,138	Dentists
83,311	Pharmacists

The health insurance system handles an enormous number of claims every year. The insurance fund for employees, for example, handled 517,351,000 claims in 1985. Through an extensive computer system, all claims are processed and paid two months after the service is provided. Other systems monitor claims for omissions and errors. As in all systems everywhere, there is potential for abuse. Medical bills are calculated according to a fee schedule of points prescribed by Chuikyo (Central Social Insurance Medical Council). In 1986, points claimed for payment were reduced by third party monitors at a rate of 0.012 percent. This rather modest rejection rate is an indication of a low rate of abuse not unlike other aspects of Japanese society. In other words, the system works within a very high degree of honesty.

Re-Evaluation and Reform

As already noted, the basic structure of the National Health Insurance system was first implemented in 1922. At that time, there were 56 million Japanese and 5 percent were 65 years or older. In 1987, there were 122 million Japanese and 11.2 percent were aged. By 1990, the percent of persons 65 years or older will climb to 16.3 percent.

This dramatic demographic change is placing a burden on a system primarily designed for a much younger constituency. Older people are, of course, more intensive users of health care systems and services. The nature of medical services has also undergone a transformation. Diagnostic tests and treatment procedures are far more sophisticated and expensive than they were in the past.

Accommodating these additional expenses within the framework of the present system will undoubtedly require financial resources beyond government's ability or willingness to pay. There is, therefore, a need to re-evaluate and reform the system. Many ideas are currently being brought forward by interested parties both inside and outside government. Some expenses will be reduced, others will be increased, and others will be reallocated.

Forging a consensus for reform will require new thinking, innovations and leadership. There is no model that the Japanese can borrow from another country, modify to suit their own needs, and instantly implement as a new system. Other systems in other countries do not appear to offer solutions.

For this and other reasons the Japanese approach to the problem is worthy of attention elsewhere. One can be cautiously optimistic the Japanese will develop a new framework within which they can continue to improve the level of health care at an affordable cost. Equality of health care for everyone has been achieved. To raise the quality of health care for young and old alike is now the challenge. Solutions applied in Japan may be worth emulating in other countries facing similar problems.

III

Japan Beginning to License Out

Chapter 11

R&D BREAKOUT

No one can ignore the rapid pace of high-tech R&D achievements in Japan. Innovative research can no longer be considered the exclusive domain of American and European laboratories. This leap to center stage paralleled the strengthening of patent laws, a shift from process to basic research, and the increased commitment of resources to R&D. Small-step innovation characterizes the process. Market niches, unexploited by foreign firms, are filled. End results are proving cost-effective.

We have been lulled into believing Japanese researchers could only copy achievements made in U.S. or European laboratories. The word "copy" in this context is not a compliment, it is a dirty word. When Europeans accused Americans of this practice in the late 19th century, the Americans invented a new term for what they were doing. It was called "Yankee ingenuity."

This is an attitude problem which may blind Americans to real achievements made in laboratories outside their own sphere of influence. An effective competitive response is not possible if Americans do not have proper respect for the potential power of their competition. High-tech companies are driven by new products. For a number of years, more new chemical entities have originated from Japan than from any other single country. An outdated notion of copying is no longer an appropriate characterization of Japanese R&D. How should it be described? A case in point is Japan's pharmaceutical research.

It is risky to describe Japan's pharmaceutical R&D establishment in statistical terms, particularly in making comparisons with other countries. No one coordinates the data and no one knows if everyone is counting the same way. Nevertheless, numbers can be revealing in the sense of giving order-of-magnitude clues to what is going on. Table 11 is an example of one effort.

At the gross spending level, U.S. firms clearly outspend their Japanese counterparts by a factor of 2.4 to 1.0. U.S. R&D expenditures as a percentage of sales are double the Japanese rate. Each country spends the same amount of money per R&D employee. Given the differential between the amount of money allocated to R&D in both countries, it is surprising that Japan approved many more new drugs in 1986 than were approved in the U.S.

This phenomenon is not unique to 1986. New chemical entities approved in the U.S. averaged twenty-one per year from 1976 to 1985. During the same period, Japan averaged thirty-six per year. It appears Japan, in the aggregate, is managing its R&D money more productively than is the U.S. That is to say, it is obtaining more products for less money.

The data, however, give no clue to the quality of the products approved. Furthermore, relative productivity is an elusive subject to measure. The data are often conflicting. For example, patents may be considered a measure of innovative research since they are the first public evidence of discoveries made by industrial laboratories. Table 12 summarizes the data for 1987. The data, at face value, indicate drug innovation is alive and well in the U.S. However, over 50 percent of U.S. drug patents were awarded to foreign companies.

When drug patent applications in Japan were looked at more closely, a surprising pattern was noted. During a six-year period ending in 1987, twenty top foreign pharmaceutical firms applied for 3,817 patents. Twenty top Japanese firms applied for 4,140 patents during the same time period.

R&D BREAKOUT

TABLE 11
Pharmaceutical Research & Development Spending — 1986

	Total ($ billion)	No. of Researchers	Per Employee ($ 000)	% of Sales	No. New Products Approved
U.S.	3.6	28,010	121.3	14.8	30
Japan	1.4	11,325	123.6	6.89	33

Note: 1. U.S.$1.00 = ¥238.54
2. Sources of data are the Pharmaceutical Manufacturers Association and the Japan Pharmaceutical Manufacturers Association.

TABLE 12
Number of Patents Related to Drugs–1987

	Total Number of Patents	Number of Patents Related to Drugs	Percent Related to Drugs
U.S.	89,489	2,358	2.6
Germany	23,640	450	1.9
Japan	62,480	1,047	1.7

TABLE 13
R&D Expenditures in Japan and the U.S.

		U.S. $ million	Percent of National Income	Percent Financed by Public Funds
Japan	1970	5,011	1.96%	25.2%
	1985	34,025	3.19	19.4
U.S.A.	1970	26,134	2.89	57.0
	1985	108,782	3.06	46.8

Note: U.S.$ = ¥238.5

By this measure, Japanese companies seem to be innovating as well as or better than their foreign competitors.

But once again the data lack an analysis of the quality of patents, and patents do not necessarily mean marketable drugs. Yet over a relatively

JAPAN BEGINNING LICENSE OUT

short time-frame, there is no denying the increased productivity of Japanese R&D. This is not restricted to drug research. The Science and Technology Agency of Japan has compiled data for R&D in all industries. A portion of the analysis is shown in Table 13.

The data indicate that over a fifteen-year period Japan has significantly increased the percentage of national income devoted to R&D. It now exceeds the U.S. rate. However, absolute expenditures are one-third the U.S. level. As noted earlier, this one-third level of spending also characterizes relative drug R&D expenditures between the two countries. While the U.S. clearly outspends Japan, much more U.S. research is paid for by the government. This raises an interesting question related to R&D productivity. R&D in Japan is primarily financed by private industry and may therefore have a more direct impact on economic competitiveness.

In this regard, the Organization for Economic Cooperation and Development Science and Technology Indicators for 1982 are of interest. The data shown in Table 14 are for all manufacturing in several countries. In terms of exported manufactured goods, all the countries listed in Table 15 have increased their R&D intensity.

Japan has become more R&D-intensive, and has moved "upstream" to compete in a wide variety of high-technology products. The pattern can be documented in a number of diverse product areas. Drugs are no exception. A "surprise-free" prediction is that Japan will be a continuing source of new drug technology, with competitive implications worldwide.

The drug industry places more emphasis on basic research than all other industries. In 1985, all industries in Japan spent 5.9 percent of their R&D money on basic research, 21.9 percent on applied research, and 72.1 percent on development. These numbers fit common wisdom, which credits the Japanese with excellent developmental capabilities but poor performance in discovering breakthrough products. However, the pharmaceutical research budget is split 17.0 percent basic, 27.3 percent applied, and 55.7 percent in development.

Nevertheless, Japanese companies are not in the same league as their international competitors. A review of seventeen foreign pharmaceutical firms indicated 75 percent of their new drugs were discovered in-house. A

R&D BREAKOUT

TABLE 14
Weights of High R&D Intensity Industries
in Total Manufacturing Output (%)

	1975	1982
Japan	12.2	13.4
U.S.A.	12.5	10.8
U.K.	11.2	12.5
West Germany	12.1	12.0
E.C.	11.3	11.7

TABLE 15
Weights of High R&D Intensity Industries
in Total Manufacturing Exports

	1975	1982
Japan	17.2	26.9
U.S.A.	24.6	31.1
U.K.	18.8	24.8
West Germany	14.6	17.7
E.C.	15.5	16.8

similar survey of Japanese firms indicated only 52 percent of their drugs were their own discoveries. In other words, 48 percent were licensed in.

Separate data on new chemical entities discovered in Japan are indicative of the lagging competitive power of Japanese firms. Over the period 1975 through 1987, original products discovered in Japan represented 32.5 percent of total domestic drug sales but only 5.0 percent of total drug sales in the U.S. These Japanese originals were pushed in Japan by strong marketing but were not competitive in the U.S. market. In many cases, they did not represent a significant improvement over existing therapy.

There is no evidence that the discovery and development of new drugs is faster in Japan than in the U.S. Estimates made in 1984 were that the time

JAPAN BEGINNING LICENSE OUT

frame was ten to sixteen years in Japan. The U.S. experience is estimated to be ten-plus years.

Comparative data on the cost of discovery and development do not exist. Cross statistics cited earlier suggested the Japanese are able to turn out a larger number of drugs at a lower cost, but the numbers may be influenced by several factors:

1. Japanese firms have a higher percentage of licensed products in their development pipeline. These products do not incur basic research expenses and the development programs benefit from data obtained elsewhere by the originator.
2. Second and third-generation drugs involve less risk in the research process and are therefore less expensive.
3. Follow-up products, even though original entities, do not break new and expensive ground in the development phase.

Elaboration on these points is warranted. The U.S. experience in R&D demonstrates an orientation toward breakthrough products, or the first generation of a new product class. Estimates indicate there is a one in 10,000 probability of success in the discovery and development of new drugs in the U.S.

A review of ten Japanese companies over a recent five-year period indicates their probability of success is one in 7,167 compounds tested. This more favorable probability factor is likely due to the Japanese orientation toward second and third-generation products, which are less risky to discover and develop than original products.

It would be shortsighted to conclude Japanese R&D is less innovative because of the above comments. We can say that the effort is different. One very good reason for the difference is simple economics. The data for sixteen major firms in Japan over the period 1975 to 1985 indicate net profit ratios of 3 to 4 percent. For twelve major firms in the U.S. the net profit ratio was 10 to 13 percent.

Japanese pharmaceutical executives have been forced to follow a less risky, less expensive R&D path because of the earning power of their sales base. Not only is the profit rate lower than in U.S. firms, the absolute amount of money available is also lower.

Furthermore, profit ratios of Japanese firms have not been improved by licensed-in products. They require less money to bring to market, but earn far less than products discovered in-house. Getting off this treadmill is a delicate balancing act of wanting the higher margins of originality but lacking the earning power to take the risks of getting there.

Another factor that forces small step innovation is the method of reimbursement for drugs under the health insurance system. Net selling prices inexorably go down. Second-generation products offer marginal medical benefits over original products, but receive higher reimbursement prices. Third-generation products follow the same pattern. Product life cycles are thereby shortened and executives must constantly refresh their product portfolios. Few products become "cash cows," characterized by stable prices, high demand, and declining promotional expenses.

R & D Facilities

In 1987, the pharmaceutical trade journal Yakuji Nippo questioned a wide range of firms in Japan about their research facilities. In Table 16, data are summarized for seventeen major companies from which several conclusions can be derived.
1. Prior to 1960, there was virtually no organized pharmaceutical industry research in Japan.
2. There was a boom in construction of R&D laboratories during the

TABLE 16
R & D Facilities (17 companies)

Year Established	No. of Facilities
1950s	4
1960s	26
1970s	28
1980s	67

1980s. More laboratories were constructed in the last eight years than were built in the previous thirty years.
3. I estimate these seventeen companies had 9,000 researchers. There were 125 separate research facilities, or on average seventy-two people per facility.

Some commentators have criticized U.S. drug research for spending more and more money for fewer products. Several specific examples are given to support the charge of research mismanagement. These accusations can be combined into two categories:
1. Success breeds conservatism, inflexibility and bureaucratic procedures.
2. Centralization inhibits innovation.

If there is any validity in these accusations, the Japanese may be home free. No blockbuster products have been discovered in Japan upon which researchers could rest on their laurels, give speeches and cease to innovate. There are no National Institutes of Health-like research facilities. The facilities are small, decentralized and new.

Of course, this is not necessarily the result of intelligent foresight on the part of Japanese R&D executives. Restricted land space in Japan does not permit the construction of large, campus-like research facilities. Lack of financial resources forces management to concentrate on small-step, risk-adverse innovation. Also, since licensed products are now more difficult to obtain, management has been forced to build up internal research resources.

On Balance

Japanese pharmaceutical R&D is new, decentralized, innovative in small steps, and is growing rapidly. In the past, weak patent protection forced emphasis on process research versus product research. The availability of licensed-in technology promoted developmental research rather than basic research. Government-mandated price reductions limit the financial resources available for R&D. Productivity, as measured by patents and licensed-out technology contracts, has increased. A construction blitz has provided an increasing number of researchers with modern, state-of-the art facilities.

Generally, all of the above are positive features of Japan's R&D establishment. In terms of sheer size, it does not match the research base of the American or European competition. Nevertheless, it demonstrates great potential and quickly responds to market needs. Foreign competitors cannot assume their leading product will be safe from second and third-generation competitors.

Not all Japanese companies are positioned in an R&D breakout mode. Many lack the critical mass to innovate. Many are trapped in a downward spiral of lower prices and no new products. In this regard, the Ministry of Health and Welfare is in a dilemma. On the one hand, it wants to protect the public welfare by reducing costs and setting strict standards for drug approval. The latter prolongs drug testing and increases research expenditures. On the other hand, it wants to foster a research-intensive, internationally competitive industry through incentives for research and a moderation of price reductions. These are often opposing objectives, resulting in a lack of leadership and an unclear set of national goals.

Negative forces are also at work inside the industry. Firms often fail to attract the best people, who prefer the status and prestige of academic research laboratories. Also, virtually all research is carried out in Japan by Japanese, depriving researchers of the cross-cultural stimulus to innovation. Personnel policies are often inflexible, old-fashioned, and bureaucratic. Knowledge of regulatory requirements outside Japan is often lacking, inhibiting rapid diffusion of original products to foreign markets.

U.S. Company Response

Japan is and will be a source of innovative drugs. The evidence for this statement is so persuasive it cannot be ignored. As of now, Japanese companies are not positioned properly to exploit the fruits of their research in international markets. American company alliances with innovative Japanese firms can result in mutually profitable sales in other countries.

JAPAN BEGINNING LICENSE OUT

However, this is a short-term opportunity that will vanish as Japanese firms establish operations outside Japan.

At present, few U.S. companies with a presence in Japan have the facilities or people to conduct basic research. The good news is that many more are planning to establish this capability in the near future. In fact, by the early 1990s, two-thirds of U.S. firms in Japan will be conducting basic research.

A research presence in Japan can be productive; many firms believe it is essential. Successful companies do not impose a strict cloning of their U.S. R&D procedures on Japanese researchers. Much can be learned from successful local methods. The secret is to build on strength. Both systems have worked in their own way; blending the two is synergistic. As foreign firms learn to do basic research in Japan, Japanese firms will be setting up research bases in the U.S. and Europe to also learn.

Research collaboration is also a largely unexplored option for U.S. firms in Japan. Productive arrangements require from both sides a willingness to communicate openly and freely. It is a process most find difficult to manage, but has potential for mutual gain. During my tenure in Japan, I have been involved in research collaborations between two U.S. and six Japanese firms. Those that worked best were well defined in a specific area of research; had definitive target dates for completing the work; held formal review meetings on a planned, periodic basis; and had lead researchers on both sides who had mutual respect for each other.

When a U.S. firm licenses a product to a Japanese company, it should stay very close to the development process, communicating regularly and asking for as much information as possible. This can be an invaluable learning experience in developing and registering a product in Japan, but the opportunity has often been neglected.

American firms can also work closely with academic institutions and their researchers, who are familiar with the achievements of U.S. laboratories. Collaborative efforts are often welcomed. Japanese firms are now funding some research in U.S. institutions. These moves are worth emulating in Japan.

R&D BREAKOUT

Since 1970, I have been impressed with Japanese researchers' dedication. They rarely change jobs, and thus preserve for their employers the benefits of training, postgraduate education, and experience. Over time, I have noticed a growing sense of confidence among these people. They are willing to learn and dream realistically of elevating their company research to an international level of excellence. If this goal is realized, everyone will benefit.

A stream of new products is the lifeblood of high-tech firms. Forming strategic alliances with Japanese companies that have a productive R&D effort can be a win/win game. A prerequisite is mutual respect for the capabilities of the other party. Japanese R&D achievements in recent years are not a "here today, gone tomorrow" phenomenon.

Bringing a product out of the laboratory is an important event but not the last step in competing effectively in Japan. Marketing a product successfully provides the returns necessary to continue the search for new innovations. An aspect of high-tech marketing strategy is explored in the next chapter. Innovation is not the sole prerogative of scientists. New marketing techniques are being employed in Japan to increase market share and prolong product life cycles. Keeping pace with the competition requires new ways of thinking, in the laboratory and in the field.

Chapter 12

THE CO-DEVELOPMENT/CO-MARKETING BOOM

> *Co-development and co-marketing agreements are now booming. Exclusivity, once so near and dear to the heart of marketing executives, is an old-fashioned idea not suited to practical market realities. This dramatic shift in strategy is now a fact of business life in the Japanese pharmaceutical market, driven by escalating product development costs, active licensing programs, and the need for critical mass in a diverse market. Companies try to make it a win/win game.*

During the 1970s, drugs were developed by one company and subsequently sold by one company. Exclusivity was considered the only way to write a licensing agreement. Co-marketing was a "dirty word" to sales executives. Co-development was demeaning to researchers. Co-anything conjured up visions of a slowdown in development, price wars, and slicing a sales pie into small pieces. No one counted the number of co-marketing and co-development agreements because there were so few to count, an insignificant factor in the pharmaceutical business.

Recently, everyone is counting and the list grows longer each year. In 1986, the journal Detailman published a special article on co-marketed and co-developed drugs. Its data indicated that in 1985, fifty-one different drugs were being co-marketed by a total of forty-one different companies.

THE CO-DEVELOPMENT/CO-MARKETING BOOM

In 1986, 166 drugs were being co-developed by 133 different companies. As co-developed drugs are brought to market it is safe to assume the number of co-marketers will significantly increase. In other words, in a short time span the number of companies involved in collaborative efforts increased threefold.

The practice has become so widespread that virtually every American and Japanese drug company is now engaged in at least one co-development or co-marketing program. As relationships of this sort are established between companies, the process leads to future collaboration and continued expansion of a phenomenon not taken seriously in the recent past.

Rationale

Market Coverage. Nine leading drug companies in Japan were analyzed to determine coverage of physicians in hospitals (100 beds or more) and general practice (under 100 beds). Table 17 summarizes the data.

The companies selected had detail forces ranging from 400 to 1,400 men, yet the highest coverage of the total market was 27 percent. On average, it was 20 percent. These "low" numbers reflect the intensity of detailing in Japan, the concentration of the sales force on key doctors, and the role of wholesaler salesmen in promoting to G.P.s.

The same nine companies work with 155 to 200 different wholesalers. As expected, actual business volume is concentrated within a more limited

TABLE 17
Physician Coverage

	H.P.	G.P.	Total
No. of institutions	4,631	83,815	88,506
No. of physicians	129,000	113,000	242,000
Highest	49%	9%	27%
Average	33%	7%	20%
Lowest	15%	3%	9%

list of wholesalers with the mean around eighty wholesalers accounting for 80 percent of the business. The wholesalers' role is not limited to order-taking and physical distribution. They actively promote drugs to doctors and thereby extend the coverage of manufacturers in the market. Another option to increase coverage is expansion of the number of medical representatives. Common wisdom indicates a force of 600 men is the critical mass required to achieve respectable coverage of the market. There is, however, an upper limit to this option imposed by financial and management control constraints. Companies with approximately 1,500 medical representatives would appear to have reached this limit.

Increasing sales force productivity is another option to increase coverage of the market. Training programs, physician seminars, advertising, and new methods of communicating product information are examples of this approach. Other companies structure themselves as "niche players" by concentrating on certain therapeutic specialties and the physician specialists in these areas, e.g., ophthalmology and ophthalmologists.

Nevertheless, given all the above efforts, companies perceive co-marketing as a cost-effective answer to achieving rapid market penetration and longer, sustained market presence. This is particularly true if each of the collaborators has specific market segment strengths. They may be geographical, i.e., east as opposed to west Japan; or by hospital size, i.e., large hospitals versus G.P.s; or via physician specialty.

Problems arise when there is overlapping of territories between medical representatives and they compete for the same business. One solution is the establishment of a clear division of labor during the development phase, particularly Phase II and Phase III studies. Good communication must also exist between the co-marketing companies at all levels. Since there is ample room in the market, minimizing territory conflicts is not an impossible or illegal task. Different trade names and packaging are also utilized effectively to distinguish product identity.

In another study, products exclusively developed and marketed were compared with products co-developed and co-marketed. Four product categories were selected: cardiovascular, anti-inflammatory, injectable cephalosporins, and oral cephalosporins. The results indicate:

THE CO-DEVELOPMENT/CO-MARKETING BOOM

1. There is no evidence of either approach resulting in a higher initial NHI price, or
2. Faster price erosion of NHI prices.

There is, however, some evidence to indicate co-marketed products do:
1. Have wider and more rapid market penetration, and
2. Sustain market share longer.

The data did not clearly substantiate the above conclusions since the sample of cases was small, simply because the phenomenon is so new. However, future analysis will be very instructive in confirming these early indications.

Development. The cost of development beyond the discovery phase varies by product. No adequate data are available in Japan to give even estimated costs. One can generalize by saying the costs are not small, probably on the order of 5 to 10 billion yen, and are increasing rapidly, Everyone agrees it is preferable to conduct as many clinical studies as possible in a wide range of indications, and in a large number of institutions over a broad geographical area.

Publicized results of clinical studies indicate that in antibiotic development programs 500 institutions and 3,000 clinical cases are not unusual numbers. It is also known that the process does not simply involve a letter to an investigator asking for his cooperation, forwarding clinical trial samples, and receiving by mail the results of the study. It is an intensive process of first convincing a "boss" to organize a study team; of personally calling upon each investigator at regular intervals; of holding investigator meetings; and finally organizing the results.

The development staff in a single company may or may not be up to this task. Consideration must also be given to time. A delay in registration is an enormous opportunity cost and must be avoided. A review of actual examples of co-developed products indicated that there is no hard evidence that co-development speeded up the registration process. An argument can be made that the additional coordination required between two companies actually delays the process. In fact, it seems to be a wash, neither faster nor slower than single-company development.

Quite clearly, however, co-development results in significantly wider exposure during the development phase, that is, more studies at more institutions. The value of this was noted above—wider and faster initial market penetration.

Japan's Ministry of Health and Welfare has simplified certain procedures for applications for drugs developed by multiple parties. Manufacturing license transfer procedures; changes in the country of origin; changes in the location of an importer; and stability test procedures have also been simplified. These actions have facilitated working with more than one company and no doubt have prompted foreign companies to make agreements with more than a single, exclusive agent.

A review of Japanese products licensed out to foreign companies for marketing abroad is also indicative of the trend toward non-exclusive agreements. Typically, the Japanese reserve a right for their company to conduct development and/or marketing by themselves in addition to the licensee in any specific country. On a global basis, usually several licensees are given rights for specific areas, such as the U.S., German-speaking countries, South America, etc.

Licensing. Both Japanese and American CEOs are frequently quoted as follows: "We will positively develop new drugs on a cross license basis." They are really saying, "We are not tied to any one company, we will license drugs from anyone and to anyone."

In the past, an announcement of a licensing agreement stated only the territory and the financial terms. Now, agreements often include some form of cross licensing. "We will give you one of our products if we can get one of yours." This is understandable if one considers the need for new products and the increasing cost of finding them. This is a worldwide problem but particularly acute in Japan, where the intensity of competition and the downward price spiral have shortened product life cycles. Active licensing programs—and all companies now have them—depend on the capability of offering exchange products. No longer is it an enticement to have a worldwide development capability, a significant worldwide marketing presence, or a lot of up-front money. Companies look for products to supplement their own product line, to replace aging products, or

THE CO-DEVELOPMENT/CO-MARKETING BOOM

simply because a licensed product can be brought to the market sooner than in-house candidates.

Future Directions

The boom in co-development and co-marketing agreements is so recent and has involved such a large number of companies it is difficult to isolate trends. Co-development and co-marketing agreements have involved both small and large companies; have not been confined to one country; and they span all therapeutic categories. Nevertheless, certain changes brought about by this phenomenon are predictable.

First, the co-development and co-marketing boom will most likely accelerate the demise of the joint venture as a customary mode of investment in Japan. As already noted, foreign companies are interested in receiving products for worldwide marketing in exchange for their products. Japanese companies with potential products are not interested in joint venturing as a way to receive technology.

The fundamental rationale for joint ventures has changed on both sides. Furthermore, very few joint venture companies conduct basic research, therefore they do not have product exchange possibilities. They remain totally dependent on one or both parents to give them a position with new products. This can create conflicts of interest that do not have easy solutions.

Secondly, basic research collaborations will increase. It is a natural upstream extension of the emphasis on licensing. Working jointly at an early stage will guarantee a position in the marketing of research discoveries. This type of joint effort has been carried out between academic and industry research laboratories. There are also similar agreements between pharmaceutical companies and companies in other industries, i.e. chemicals, cosmetics and foods.

One difficulty in conducting joint research between high-tech companies is the question of ownership and patent rights. This has scared off potential collaboration by some. Others have found a way to define discrete areas of research that complement the ongoing work of both parties. Also, some projects are simply too massive for an individual company to cope with alone. As experience is gained in the management of these pioneering efforts, their numbers will increase.

Thirdly, attracting products from others can result from market niche dominance. Establishing an overwhelming presence in a particular product category is a good selling point to others with product candidates but who lack the marketing skills or resources to maximize sales. As we have seen, no single company in Japan covers the entire market and the strength of each is often localized. This could lead to a rise of specialty marketing companies, just as we have seen the specialty product company become viable.

Boom and Bust?

The desire for exclusivity is not going to fade away. Companies in Japan are fond of reporting down to the tenth percentage point sales represented by products discovered in-house. Most companies obscurely footnote products licensed into the firm.

Conflicts of interest arise when a licensed-in product is overshadowed by a competitive product discovered internally. Marketing resources are shifted to emphasize "our" product. Internal reporting and reward schemes give different emphasis to products depending on their source.

Attracting innovative and creative researchers to work on other people's discoveries is a difficult task. Research management will need to find effective ways to have both original and complementary research programs operating under the same roof. Inventing is considered more attractive than developing.

A breakthrough product may quickly set aside co-development and co-marketing policies that were put in place during the lean years. Discussions of benefits from co-marketing go out the window as company executives become enamored with their own success. "Doing it my way" may not be the best way, but it is the most comfortable.

Given these facts, we might be witnessing a short-lived "blip" in the way companies conduct business. Time and experience alone will answer

THE CO-DEVELOPMENT/CO-MARKETING BOOM

this question. Meanwhile, the practical realities of the business, and the all-pervasive nature of this co-development and co-marketing boom will permanently change at least certain aspects of the industry philosophy. Change comes fastest to those who least expect it.

Success or failure in Japan's high-tech market is tied closely to the productivity of R&D efforts. Lead times in research are getting longer, product life cycles in the market are getting shorter. The costs of discovery are escalating.

Managers of research have come to appreciate that they do not have the financial resources or brains to cover all the bases. They have tried hard to eliminate from their corporate culture the "not invented here" syndrome. Marketing managers can utilize their resources to push products derived from in-house research and from another company's research, equally effectively.

Throughout the high-tech industry, a new buzz word is "generations" of products. First-generation products are supplemented by second-generation products. Third-generation products take market share from second-generation products. The innovator cannot rest on his laurels. Cash cows dry up quickly.

It is not surprising that licensing in and out has become an essential feature of staying in the game. Companies may compete fiercely in the market but carefully nurture good relations between their respective licensing departments. Strategic alliances and business collaborations are new strategies designed to maintain and enhance a competitive presence. Licensing department employees have become key players with high corporate visibility. Characteristics of this phenomenon are described in the next chapter.

Chapter 13

SUCCESSFUL LICENSING IN JAPAN OR, IS THE GAME OVER?

Suddenly the fruits of Japanese research became objects of intensive licensing-in programs by American companies. Certain factors separated winners from losers. All companies became more sophisticated in the process. Now that everyone has learned to play the game, the game itself may be over. Opportunities remain but responsibility is relegated to lawyers or corporate licensing departments. Operating managers must stay involved to extract maximum strategic value from the agreement. Signing is only the beginning.

During the late 1970s, it did not require a great deal of intelligence or insight to predict that the Japanese would discover high-tech products of useful value. The pharmaceutical industry is a prime example. Various leading indicators suggested it was only a matter of time before world-class drugs would make their appearance in Japan. Several of these indicators deserve mention since they are common to many high-tech industries.
  Number of People in R&D. In 1975, the Japanese pharmaceutical industry employed 135,759 people. Of these, 17,480 or 12.9 percent were classified as working in R&D. By 1984, total employment had increased 29 percent but those employed in R&D increased by 55 percent. To accommodate the increased number of employees, company after company announced the building of new laboratory facilities. In addition to the in-

crease in sheer space, it is safe to assume that newer facilities incorporated advances in equipment technology not available to researchers in older facilities.

A review of equipment investment trends in sixteen major companies from 1984 to 1985 indicated investment of 864 million yen and 925 million yen respectively for these two years. Eleven out of the sixteen companies indicated a major portion of their investment was utilized for research facilities. Japanese executives are shifting capital expenditures from production-related facilities to R&D.

More Money for R&D. Since 1975, R&D expenditures in the entire pharmaceutical industry have almost doubled every five years. This increase in absolute value pushed the R&D expense to sales ratio from 4.91 percent in 1975 to 6.89 percent in 1986. The trend is even more dramatic in the larger firms that are members of the Japan Pharmaceutical Manufacturers Association (JPMA). In 1986, their R&D to sales ratio stood at 10.48 percent. It should be noted that this increase occurred while the net income to sales ratio increased marginally. For fifteen leading companies, the ratio was 3.6 percent in 1975 and 4.5 percent in 1986.

The phenomenon of more money for R&D is also evident among middle-ranking ethical manufacturers. A survey of ten companies indicated their R&D to sales ratio went from 7.5 percent to 8.3 percent between 1984 and 1985. Expense increases were driven by the additional people employed, and by the increased activity of the research process, in other words, more effort in basic research.

Number of Published Patents Is Increasing. In 1978, a total of 249 patents related to drugs were issued to Japanese applicants. This represented 0.5 percent of all patents issued. In 1987, the number of drug patents issued was 618 which represented 1.0 percent of all issued patents in Japan. This is a remarkable increase in a relatively short time span and is one indication of the payback from investments in R&D.

Technology Exports Increasing. A more dramatic indication of the productivity of research in Japan is the number of contracts executed for the export of technology. In 1975, there were only sixty-three such contracts. In 1986, the number had increased to 244. Perhaps the value of exported technology is the bottom line of this analysis. In 1977, the total value of technology exported by JPMA member firms was 1.8 billion yen. In 1986, the value was 12.3 billion yen. Furthermore, by 1985 the Japanese were receiving as much revenue from exported technology as they were paying for imported technology, a turnaround from years of deficit spending in this category. If we isolate the relative value of new contracts only from the above data, exports have exceeded imports in both number and value since 1982.

Japan has shifted from being a net importer of technology to a net exporter. While it might have been easy to see it coming, few predicted it would occur so rapidly.

Response by American Companies

Japanese companies have always devoted an enormous amount of time to listening. They send teams of people to international scientific meetings in order to find out "what's new." They visit companies around the world to inquire about recent research developments. They are hospitable hosts for visiting research executives who are encouraged to report on the work being done in their laboratories back home.

This exercise in new product intelligence is not limited to one particular section of the firm. In fact, everyone seems to have a hand in the process. Study teams are made up of people from a variety of functions. The search for new products is not only the responsibility of the licensing department.

American researchers are flattered by the attention bestowed upon them. They are encouraged to talk more about their research rather than ask questions about Japanese research. Furthermore, there was (is?) a common notion that Japanese research was not worth listening to.

It is a fact that many drugs developed in Japan are not marketed in America or Europe. In 1985 for example, forty-six of the top 100 products in Japan were developed solely through the efforts of Japanese companies. Twenty-three, or half of these products, were sold only in Japan since it was considered doubtful whether approval could be obtained overseas.

SUCCESSFUL LICENSING IN JAPAN

Given the best intentions to listen, most Americans are not able to understand the Japanese language or read the literature. Meanwhile, the Japanese peruse everything written in English. Few foreign researchers know what is being published in Japanese unless it appears in an English journal. This gap in basic intelligence very much favors the Japanese firm. Researchers in America may conclude that innovation originates only on the eastern side of the Pacific Ocean.

A related problem concerns the degree of responsibility relegated to American subsidiary employees in Japan for conducting licensing work. Typically, the local R&D staff is fully preoccupied with developing products discovered by their parent company. They have no defined mission to search for products that are discovered in Japan.

An organizational response to these deficiencies is to establish and staff a unit in Japan to conduct the scientific aspects of licensing intelligence. However, this is easier said than done. Appropriate Japanese employees must be bilingual and have an in-depth knowledge of basic science as well as the research interests of the parent company. It is also a thankless task, concentrated on reading the literature and attending scientific meetings. The people must have good communication skills and be of an appropriate age to relate to senior researchers in Japanese laboratories.

Successful American companies have found it useful to have a senior, respected scientist transferred to Japan to work with the local scientific staff. It may be a person in the twilight of his career yet enthusiastic for a new challenge and particularly interested in new developments over a spectrum of scientific disciplines.

If properly staffed, and this is a big if, the unit may require years to establish relationships with Japanese firms to insure an open flow of communication. The investment does not come cheaply and objective results are often difficult to define. The firm needs patience and an ongoing commitment to the process to realize success.

Another key to a successful licensing program is the involvement of local operating management. Potential licensed-in products need to be judged by scientific and economic measurements. Enthusiasm for this function is often lacking because the local manager is primarily evaluated on business results in Japan. What he might contribute to results elsewhere, five years into the future, does not appear on year-end performance reviews.

Some companies also face a major problem in conducting fair, objective reviews of licensed-in product candidates. In this process speed is often a key factor, and there might be less than adequate information available for the review. To varying degrees, every company is inhibited by a "not invented here" syndrome, particularly if in-house product candidates are competitive to the licensed-in candidate. It takes a strong research management team to turn off these efforts in favor of a product from another company, particularly a company that is unknown to the research staff.

These comments may be summarized in a list of dos and don'ts for a successful licensing program.

Do	Don't
Respect the potential of Japanese R&D to discover products of worldwide marketing significance.	Believe the Japanese are incapable of innovation or develop products that can only be sold in Japan.
Staff a function in Japan whose sole purpose is to seek out new product candidates.	Conduct licensing by having home office personnel visit Japan and see ten companies in five days.
Commit resources to the licensing intelligence effort on a long-term basis.	Put people into licensing because you don't know where else to put them.
Involve operating managers in the licensing process. Measure and pay for results.	Have a local licensing function report to the home office licensing department on a direct-line basis.
Set internal targets for licensing candidates and establish a timely review process.	Let product candidates get a bad review simply because they were not invented here.

SUCCESSFUL LICENSING IN JAPAN

These dos and don'ts relate primarily to passing the scientific aspects of the review process. Equally important is concluding a business arrangement and getting the product to market. Few licenses result from a Japanese company knocking on the door and saying, "We have a product you should market outside Japan on the basis of your own internal financial measurements."

A review of license agreements indicates no general model exists. However, it does prove that the end result remains a matter of negotiation. Some agreements have been concluded with sizable up-front payments, others with no pre-payment. Some have involved manufacturing rights, others none. Some have involved immediate product exchanges, in others this is a matter for future negotiation. Often, the Japanese specify terms similar to those which they themselves were subjected to in the past, when they were receiving rather than giving. Some involve extensive legal agreements, others are not much more than a handshake.

What works for one company may not work in another company. Yet it is universally important to recognize that both sides must "win." Each party must respect the value of the other party's contribution and find a way to fairly share the wealth.

For both parties, time is money. A product does not move one inch closer to a paying customer as long as people are working on the contract. To some, often lawyers, this is the beginning and end of the deal. Although contract negotiations are important, since they do establish future parameters under which both sides can work most effectively, they must be conducted under a spirit of mutual respect and with a cold eye on the clock.

Some may argue the contract should cover every conceivable future scenario. This ideal is hardly ever practical, particularly when one is considering a product very early in the development cycle. It is a pragmatic procedure for the negotiators to establish broad, general principles that can be fine-tuned as future conditions warrant. Both parties must recognize that conditions do change during a development time cycle that frequently requires five years to complete.

JAPAN BEGINNING LICENSE OUT

Time spent in negotiations establishes a positive basis on which to build good working relationships. Signing an agreement is only the beginning of a process designed to bring a product into international markets. The follow-up procedures to a contract are as important as those which led to the agreement in the first place.

A short list of dos and don'ts may be illustrative of this phase of the negotiations.

Do	Don't
Expedite contract negotiations to get on with the real productive exercise of product development.	Haggle over every detail trying to win points for your side at the expense of the other's sense of net worth.
Make certain each party fully understands the basic working agreement.	Try to anticipate every possible future problem in every country.
Establish procedures for follow-up and formalize communication channels to measure results.	Sign the agreement with a flourish and then leave clerks with implementation responsibilities.
Attempt a fair understanding of the needs of the licensor.	Believe you will negotiate returns or control equal to in-house discovered products.

It is not my objective to define successful negotiation strategies. Suffice it to say that the sheer number of signed contracts indicates a lot of experience has been accumulated, both good and bad. During the five-year period from 1981 to 1985, there were 1,750 licensing contracts executed for both the import and export of pharmaceutical technology, for example. There are many people out there who are getting the job done, one way or another.

Common sense suggests that companies have become more sophisticated in the process. On average, an agreement is executed somewhere in Japan every day of the week except Sunday and national holidays. Executive recruiters are always on assignments to recruit people for licensing departments. CEOs visiting Japan do not pass up an opportunity to express their willingness to license products, both into and out of Japan.

As a result of all this activity, Japanese researchers are now flattered by the attention they are receiving. After years of asking for a product, they find themselves on the opposite side of the table. Possibly this has caused some to assume an arrogant attitude toward some outsiders. Americans are listening more and finding effective means to identify product candidates early in the development cycle. More people are walking on a two-way street with a degree of mutual, if sometimes grudging, respect.

Is the Game Over?

Although it is clear that everyone has learned to play the licensing game, it is difficult to determine the future direction of license agreements in Japan. Factual data are not useful since the number of licensing agreements is more a reflection of past events than a predictor of future trends. In fact, the actual number of licensing agreements consummated has remained relatively constant.

By many measures I have concluded there is not a slowdown in the number of new drugs being developed. For example, in 1984, a total of 105 drugs entered clinical trials. In 1985, the number was 128 drugs. In 1987, there were forty-five drugs with new ingredients (NCEs) that were approved for manufacture or import; twenty-five of these were discovered in Japan.

There are also more players in the field. In the period from January to October 1986, a total of 117 pharmaceutically-related businesses were newly licensed, sixty-six for manufacturing and fifty-one for importing. As of the end of October 1986, there were 2,298 businesses licensed for drug manufacturing and 597 for drug importing.

Given the number of drugs and the number of manufacturers, one must assume that licensing is not going to fade away overnight. On the other hand, several factors indicate the game will change.

JAPAN BEGINNING LICENSE OUT

R&D Productivity Leads Worldwide Market Presence. At present, innovative Japanese pharmaceutical companies do not have a marketing presence in international markets. In view of this fact, licensing is a measure of last resort, either license the product or forego sales opportunities outside Japan. This is not a new phenomenon unique to Japanese companies. The pattern has been seen before. Start with licensing, move to exporting, and then to an international presence.

It is logical to assume that Japanese companies with innovative research efforts will not be content with royalties or the profits garnered through manufacturing alone. Moving downstream toward full integration is economically so persuasive that we can assume it is only a question of time before these companies move offshore. Licensing out products will diminish accordingly.

Manufacturing Outside Japan. As products are established by licensees we can expect the Japanese to move some portion of manufacturing offshore. This process will be driven by high taxes, land prices and labor costs in Japan, plus a desire to be closer to market needs. A license to manufacture by an American firm is not likely under these and other economic conditions.

Customer Service is a Japanese Passion. Experience in Japan has taught Japanese competitors the value of intensive customer contact. Given this experience, it is unlikely management will continue to delegate this function to third parties.

Expanded Sales Base for an Expanded R&D Base. The market in Japan is very large but no single market can support the kind of R&D base Japanese companies are putting in place. As their American and European predecessors have already learned, the firm must have a marketing presence in Japan, Europe and America. Licensing out simply delays the inevitable.

It is safe to assume that Japanese managers will learn from the experience of others. American companies built a presence in Europe. European companies built a presence in America. Both now realize that a major presence is also necessary in Japan. Staying outside Japan and licensing into the market via a third party was a risk-avoidance, short-term strategy no longer considered viable on a long term basis.

SUCCESSFUL LICENSING IN JAPAN

At this juncture, one cannot help but note the number of licensing agreements in which Japanese companies reserve the right of eventually marketing by themselves in the licensee's country. Japanese companies are also establishing product development capabilities off shore. As these become operative, products will be licensed out for marketing only, and most likely on a non-exclusive basis.

During the 1980s, American companies learned to respect the growing productivity of Japanese R&D. They then embarked on a licensing blitz. Once again the environment is changing as Japanese companies move offshore. Licensing activity may not slow down, but the nature of the game is changing. Recognizing this and acting accordingly will separate future winners from losers.

In the past, as licensing activity increased, many firms centralized the licensing function in corporate headquarters, effectively stripping line operating managers of any power or responsibility to be part of the process. As a result, many of the people now responsible for licensing are primarily interested in "doing a deal," but have no feel for the impact on local operating environments.

Strategic alliances may replace what we now know as licensing agreements. The driving force of these agreements will not be a contract or a cross-licensing agreement. It may be termed a "business collaboration." The operative word here is business and an agreement is only the beginning in creating value for both parties.

For example, Marion Laboratories in the United States has grown rapidly and recently agreed to merge with a pharmaceutical subsidiary of Dow Chemical to create a new entity that will be one of the top ten pharmaceutical companies in the U.S. In their 1987 annual report, they spoke of a relationship with the Japanese company Tanabe Seiyaku Co., Ltd. in the following terms:

> "Tanabe-Marion Laboratories (TML), established in 1984, is the most significant business collaboration in our company's history. It provides Marion a direct access to a major pharmaceutical research operation. Tanabe, in turn, gains access to the United States and Canada through Marion's proven development and marketing resources. The needs of

each company can be met while ensuring that the individual identity of each can be maintained. It is a relationship built on mutual respect and harmony."

Licensing will survive if it remains sensitive to the needs of business managers and is not pre-empted by lawyers or corporate licensing specialists. A partnership needs continuous attention and a listening ear. Eliminating local responsibility for this function stalls the process.

Licensing can be an effective bridge over which firms can establish long-term, mutually productive alliances. This is a new challenge brought about by a Japanese presence in many international markets. Licensing, in its present form, will not persist. Innovative firms will shift their licensing strategies toward fundamental alliances, conceived, agreed to, and implemented by operating managers.

The basis for effective alliances is preconditioned on establishing a presence in each of the major high-tech markets, that is, Japan, the U.S. and Europe. To compete in Japan, a firm must be in Japan. This simple truth is often overlooked as American companies attempt to run their Japanese business from a corporate office in New York.

IV

Competing in Japan

Chapter 14

PHARMACEUTICAL WHOLESALING — LIFE IN THE FAST LANE

Virtually all prescription drugs are distributed in Japan by wholesalers. It is a tough, demanding occupation not recommended for the fainthearted. Customers want daily, fast service and semi-annual, slow payments. Manufacturers push for sales. The business is not glamorized in the media. Government bureaucrats request data and cooperation. Wholesalers are an integral part of the pharmaceutical business and every aspect of their business is changing. Fewer survivors will alter the nature of competition and distribution.

In 1954 Peter Drucker wrote a book entitled *The Practice of Management*. He made an important observation: "Creating a customer is the ultimate purpose of a business, indeed, of economic activity." In 1985, Drucker was echoing the same theme in his book *Innovation and Entrepreneurship*. He wrote:

"Above all, we know that an entrepreneurial strategy has more chance of success the more it starts out with the users — their utilities, their values, their realities. An innovation is a change in market or society. It produces a greater yield for the user, greater wealth-producing capacity for society, higher value or greater satisfaction. The test of an innovation is always what it does for the user."

COMMETING IN JAPAN

For over 30 years a persistent theme has permeated management textbooks — know your customer. Often American firms operating in Japan do not know their customers. Two factors are responsible:

1. The pharmaceutical industry employs approximately 42,000 medical representatives. U.S. firms account for about 12 percent of this total. A few successful companies account for the majority of these employees. There are 180,000 practicing physicians in Japan. Simple arithmetic suggests most U.S. firms directly contact a small percentage of end users through their own sales force.
2. Many U.S. firms have relegated customer contact to Japanese manufacturers through license agreements or joint venture contracts. While this strategy expanded the sales base of innovative products, it left U.S. firms vulnerable to competitive products developed by their Japanese distributors.

This lack of customer contact forces U.S. firms to position their products in the Japanese market based upon experience of user needs in other markets. What is deemed attractive by physicians in the U.S. is assumed to be attractive to Japanese physicians. Successful companies have learned this is not a universal truth. Marketing innovation in Japan, which begins with product development, can only be enhanced by greater knowledge of the Japanese user.

Many companies are now taking actions to increase the size of their sales force. This process requires a persistent effort over a very long time. There is no short-term solution.

In parallel with actions taken to increase the frequency and quality of direct contact with physicians, it is important to consider the role of pharmaceutical wholesalers in Japan. These organizations, estimated to number 2,000, distribute 99 percent of all prescription drugs to hospitals, dispensing physicians and pharmacies. Virtually all drugs sold by manufacturers in Japan are delivered to wholesalers, which in turn solicit specific orders from consumers.

Wholesalers in the U.S. are also an important channel to end users. Their percentage share of sales is increasing. In 1985, wholesalers represented 67.3 percent of manufacturers' sales, up more than 40 percent

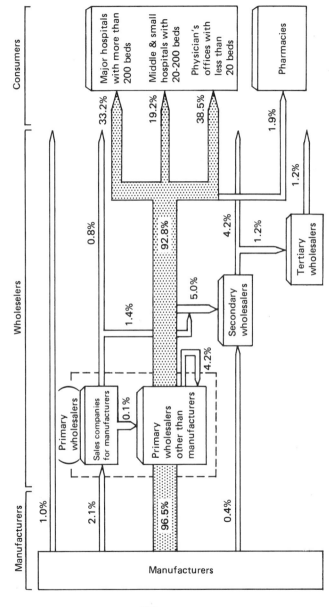

CHART 1
Distribution Channels for Prescription Drugs

from the 1975 level of 46.9 percent. Some U.S. companies rely exclusively on wholesalers, others sell direct, and others combine both approaches to the user. In Japan there is only one option — selling through wholesalers.

Unfortunately, having one channel does not imply the distribution system is simple. Chart 1 describes a portion of the complexity. There are primary, secondary and tertiary wholesalers. There are different types of consumers classified as major hospitals with more than 200 beds, middle and small hospitals with 20 to 200 beds; physician's offices with less than 20 beds, and pharmacies. The percentage numbers are estimates of prescription drug sales by all wholesalers as calculated by the Ministry of Health and Welfare.

Wholesaler Scale

The large number of wholesalers, and the fact that no single wholesaler has national distribution, adds to the complexity. However, the situation becomes somewhat more manageable by recognizing several important factors.

Scale measured by sales. Table 18 plots the percentage of firms by monthly sales for the years 1981 through 1985. This study involved 460 wholesalers. Each end of the spectrum is of greatest interest. The smallest companies with monthly sales under 10 million yen represented 18.6 percent of the total in 1981 but only 10.9 percent in 1985. On the other hand, firms with 2 billion yen sales or more per month, went from 2.8 percent to 6.5 percent of the total in the same period. A point will be made later that the total number of wholesalers is decreasing and those with sales under 10 million yen per month appear to be particularly vulnerable to a "going out of business" scenario. Note: For both Table 18 and 19 the following code is applicable.

5A Sales over 2 billion yen/m
4A Sales over 1 billion yen/m
3A Sales over 500 million yen/m
2A Sales over 300 million yen/m

1A Sales over 100 million yen/m
B Sales over 50 million yen/m
C Sales over 30 million yen/m
D Sales over 10 million yen/m
E Less than 10 million yen/m

PHARMACEUTICAL WHOLESALING

TABLE 18

Number of Companies

(% of Cos.)

	5A	4A	3A	2A	1A	B	C	D	E	Total
1981	2.8	6.3	13.0	7.3	14.6	8.1	7.7	21.3	18.6	100.0
1982	4.2	7.0	15.5	6.6	14.8	6.3	7.1	20.8	17.3	100.0
1983	5.5	8.0	14.0	8.0	14.9	5.3	9.5	21.1	13.2	100.0
1984	6.5	8.0	14.5	8.0	14.2	6.5	9.5	19.9	12.4	100.0
1985	6.5	8.7	14.4	7.7	14.2	6.9	8.9	21.4	10.9	100.0

Table 18 indicates the process of concentration within large wholesalers. Companies with monthly sales greater than 2 billion yen accounted for 48.2 percent of all sales in 1985, up from 32 percent in 1981.

TABLE 19

% of Total Prescription Drug Sales

	5A	4A	3A	2A	1A	B	C	D	E	Total
1981	32.0	25.1	23.9	7.8	7.4	1.5	0.8	1.1	0.3	100.0
1982	38.0	22.7	24.4	5.7	6.4	1.0	0.6	0.9	0.2	100.0
1983	44.2	21.6	19.9	6.3	5.5	0.7	0.7	0.8	0.2	100.0
1984	47.7	20.0	19.5	5.7	4.8	0.8	0.7	0.7	0.2	100.0
1985	48.2	21.2	18.4	5.2	4.5	0.8	0.5	0.7	0.1	100.0

The data given above indicate that wholesalers with monthly sales greater than 500 million yen accounted for 30 percent of the total number of companies, but almost 90 percent of total sales in 1985. Small wholesalers with sales under 30 million yen per month accounted for almost one-third of the companies but only 0.8 percent of total sales. This type of analysis identifies wholesalers which are surviving and serving their customers effectively.

COMMETING IN JAPAN

Number of Wholesalers. The Japan Pharmaceutical Wholesalers' Association is a nationwide organization with a central office in Tokyo. Its membership accounts for 95-plus percent of all wholesaler sales. Table 20 indicates that over a 21-year period the number of member firms decreased by 60 percent. The number of separate branches decreased by one-third. The rate of consolidation continues unabated and the association expects the number of wholesalers to decrease by one-half over the next five years.

Type of Sales. Table 21 is an analysis of wholesaler sales by member companies of the Japan Pharmaceutical Wholesalers' Association. In 1965, prescription drugs represented one-half of the business. By 1985 the percentage had grown to just under 85 percent.

Number of Employees. JPWA executives estimate their member firms employed 75,000 people in 1987. A detailed study of 99 top wholesalers (by sales ranking) revealed an employment level of 53,029 people in 1987. It also was interesting to note that the top ten companies in this sample accounted for 36.2 percent of sales, but only 33.2 percent of the employees. The top twenty companies accounted for 51.6 percent of sales and 47.4 percent of employees.

This and other data indicate that leading wholesalers are rationalizing their operations to reduce employment levels. The cost of maintaining one salesman in the field is estimated to be 10 million yen per year. This includes all costs, i.e., salary, benefits, transportation and allowances. Typically, sales personnel in wholesalers represent 50 percent of total employment.

Increased personnel costs are driving wholesalers to rationalize their operations. Personnel expenses account for more than 60 percent of operating expenses. Evidence exists that positive results have been obtained by a wide range of wholesalers. Data from 130 wholesalers for the year beginning October 1985 through September 1986 indicate sales growth of 6.07 percent but a profit increase of 9.91 percent. Other factors contributed to this positive profit performance but efforts to reduce labor costs are paying off on the bottom line.

Manufacturers Presence. In July 1987, a study was conducted on "The Actual Situation and Mid-Term Prospects of Pharmaceutical Com-

TABLE 20
JPWA Member Wholesalers

Year	Branches	Head offices
1965	1,200	1,330
1966	1,104	921
1968	1,084	866
1970	1,059	820
1972	1,006	728
1974	1,007	690
1976	965	545
1978	939	615
1980	913	577
1982	882	538
1984	832	491

TABLE 21

Year	Prescription Drugs
1965	49.5 (%)
1970	72.7
1975	78.6
1990	82.9
1985	84.9

panies." The results were published in December 1987 by Kokusai Shogyo Shuppan K.K. In this study, 117 leading wholesalers were asked to identify the top four or five manufacturers whose products led sales performance in each firm. Table 22 summarizes the results. The numbers represent the times each manufacturer was mentioned as being a sales leader.

These data are problematical because they do not indicate the amount of sales, only the mention of a leading position. The survey, however, is indicative of relative sales power. On that basis, several observations are warranted.

TABLE 22
Leading Manufacturers as Mentioned by Wholesalers (July 1987)

1.	Takeda	53	23.	Rohto	4
2.	Fujisawa	50	24.	Meiji Nyugyo	3
3.	Eisai	48	25.	Tsumura Jyuntendo	2
4.	Sankyo	45	26.	Tokyo Tanabe	2
5.	Yamanouchi	44	27.	Nippon Kayaku	2
6.	Daiichi	37	28.	Toyama	2
7.	Chugai	32	29.	Kyorin	2
8.	Tanabe	30	30.	Ono	2
9.	Shionogi	25	31.	Bristol-Myers	1
10.	Otsuka	23	32.	Hoechst Japan	1
11.	Taiho	20	33.	Smith Kline Fujisawa	1
12.	Banyu	19	34.	Zeria	1
13.	Green Cross	18	35.	Torii	1
14.	Sumitomo	18	36.	Iwaki	1
15.	Dainippon	13	37.	Nippon Vicks	1
16.	Kowa	12	38.	Kaken	1
17.	Kyowa Hakko	9	39.	Hisamitsu	1
18.	Meiji Seika	8	40.	Nippon Zoki	1
19.	Mochida	6	41.	Morishita	1
20.	Yoshitomi	6	42.	Nikken	
21.	Pfizer Taito	4	43.	Hoei	1
22.	Toyo Jyozo	4	44.	Ciba Gigy	1

1. Foreign companies rarely have a leading position in any given wholesaler. One exception is Banyu with nineteen mentions, a company majority-owned by Merck & Co., Inc.
2. In the prescription drug market, Shionogi is the first or second company as measured by market share, yet is mentioned by only twenty-five of the 117 wholesalers. This indicates concentration of effort does have benefits.
3. Historically, companies like Eisai, Yamanouchi, Daiichi and Chugai

PHARMACEUTICAL WHOLESALING

did not have strong wholesaler relations. Recently, this situation has changed.

Pricing Mechanism. Chart 2 is a generalization, and an old adage must apply, i.e., "All generalizations are false, including this one." The numbers speak for themselves and will vary depending on the product and each manufacturer's policy. However, the basic structure of the pricing mechanism prompts several comments:

1. The earning power of wholesalers centers on rebates from the manufacturers, thereby reducing autonomy.
2. The selling margin, 4 percent to 5 percent, can rapidly erode through pressure exerted by consumers.
3. The above two factors place wholesalers in the classic role of a sandwich, squeezed between supplier and customer.

CHART 2
Typical Wholesaler Pricing Mechanism

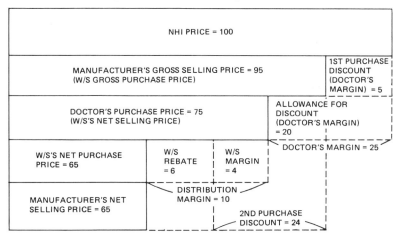

Financial Scale. The profitability of wholesalers depends on a variety of factors. In surveying over 400 wholesalers the following trends are evident:

COMMETING IN JAPAN

Higher Profitability	**Lower Profitability**
Companies located in West Japan.	Companies located in East Japan.
Monthly sales above 2 billion yen.	Monthly sales less than 2 billion yen.
High ratio of prescription drug sales.	High ratio of OTC product sales.
High ratio of sales to hospitals.	High ratio of sales to general practitioners.
High margin suppliers.	Low margin suppliers.
New products dominate portfolio.	Old products dominate portfolio.
Frequent NHI price reductions.	Infrequent NHI price reductions.
Collection periods less than four months.	Collection periods greater than four months.
Product gross margin greater than 14 percent of sales.	Product gross margin less than 14 percent of sales.
Operating expense less than 12.5 percent of sales.	Operating expense greater than 12.5 percent of sales.
Operating income greater than 0.7 percent of sales.	Operating income less than 0.7 percent of sales.
Inventory turnover less than one month.	Inventory turnover greater than one month.
Growth rate of sales per employee greater than sales growth rate.	Growth rate of sales per employee less than sales growth rate.

Rationalization. As indicated previously, the number of wholesalers has decreased rapidly. On closer examination the decrease is not as dramatic as the pattern of restructuring or the manner in which it has occurred. In historical perspective it is evident that very few wholesalers simply go out of business. Typically, they merge and create a single surviving entity. Outright acquisitions or bankruptcies played a minor role in the restructuring process.

Another phenomenon is a wave-like effect. The first wave occurred at the time of the oil crisis in the early 1970s as rapid inflation pushed labor costs beyond the capability of small wholesalers to adjust. Mergers resulted as more profitable enterprises "saved" their less profitable partners. In this manner employees were protected and few were let go.

Following this period, wholesalers merged because of positive internal business reasons, rather than from outside economic pressures. For example, two wholesalers with different customers could solidify their market base and reduce duplicating overhead expenses.

Since the early 1980s, severe price reductions mandated by the National Health Insurance system have forced another wave of consolidation. Mergers and business tie-ups were seen as a way to lower personnel costs and introduce effective management practices. Expansion of geography was a secondary issue.

Now the wholesaler industry is entering another phase of consolidation driven by a desire to expand market presence over a wider geographical area. Lessons learned in rationalizing operations at a local level, are applied over a wider area without a corresponding increase in overhead expense. A major factor is the application of integrated information networks for order solicitation and processing. Expansion of the system is cost effective and results in lower personnel costs. Small and medium sized wholesalers without this capability are not competitive, particularly as downward pressure is applied on prices and margins.

Political pressure is also being applied to modernize distribution. Model sales contracts, Fair Trade Commission actions to promote free and fair competition, correction of non-price competition, and administrative guidance are examples of the procedures being applied. No wholesaler will be immune from internal and external pressures to modernize and provide efficient service at a lower cost.

Response by Foreign Firms

In many respects the changes occurring in the wholesaler industry are positive. Fewer, more efficient, independent wholesalers will be more accessible to foreign firms. The entire system will be more transparent and rational. Aggressive, professional managers of wholesalers welcome new business relationships and the opportunity to expand their product portfolios.

It is important to understand the dynamics of the market. JPWA member wholesalers (approximately 400) control virtually all prescription drug sales to customers. These firms probably have close to 50,000 salesmen in the field. Their knowledge of the market is invaluable and they are fiercely competitive. I have never met a wholesaler executive without a calculator in his pocket.

A review of major Japanese manufacturers indicates they do about 80 percent of their business with eighty different wholesalers. The old 80:20 rule seems to apply. Eighty wholesalers represent 20 percent of the total JPWA membership. Therefore, 80 percent of the business is with 20 percent of the wholesalers. Selecting the "right" 20 percent is not an easy task, but several successful approaches are evident:

Try to	Avoid
Approach wholesalers fully recognizing they are the single channel to customers. You need them more than they need you. They are able to "push" products through the system.	A belief that if your detailmen convince doctors to use the product, wholesalers must follow. Avoid an exclusive "pull-through" strategy.

PHARMACEUTICAL WHOLESALING

Try to	**Avoid**
Concentrate on a select group of wholesalers with wide geographic distribution capabilities.	Dealing with every interested wholesaler. More is not better. Avoid competition between wholesalers.
Devote resources to establishing a "wet" relationship with wholesaler salesmen. They know your customer.	Remaining aloof from wholesaler salesmen. They talk to doctors more often than your own medical representatives.
Train wholesaler salesmen with the same intensity you train your own representatives.	An attitude that wholesaler salesmen are only order takers.

Pharmaceutical wholesalers do not survive by discovering new products. They are not protected by government subsidies or regulations. Every day they are under pressure to sell more for less. At times, outside economic pressures shrink margins and force consolidation. The winners are responsive to customer needs. They innovate and face adversity with optimism. The survivors are not blindly devoted to a single manufacturer.

U.S. companies have often delegated or forfeited responsibility for wholesalers to Japanese distributors. Knowing your customer begins with an active program to solicit the advice, enthusiasm and commitment of wholesalers. Successful companies are demonstrating the distribution system is neither mysterious nor impenetrable. Wholesalers are the key to unlocking the door. Through them you will know your customer, and that is the only legitimate basis for a successful business in Japan.

Even with good intentions, getting into Japan has never been easy or inexpensive. A common entry mode for high-tech firms has been the joint venture. The future of this type of organization is considered in the next chapter.

Chapter 15

THE JOINT VENTURE — GOING, GOING, GONE

Joint ventures, once the only feasible mode of entry into Japan, subsequently embraced as good business decisions, are now going into the history books. Born in compromise, nurtured with reluctance, never given full adult responsibilities, some of them surprisingly prospered. Many more became an exercise in mediocrity. Others have been abandoned or their structures altered. Management of these ventures consumed an unwarranted amount of time, money and people. The lessons learned should not be forgotten.

The following analysis of joint ventures in the pharmaceutical industry is not completely unbiased. Since 1970, it has been my pleasure and pain to work with seven joint ventures, three of which I was responsible for starting. Another three I closed down. There were eight Japanese parent companies and four U.S. corporations involved in the ventures. The number of employees ranged from two to 2,000. Closing down a joint venture was far more difficult than starting one. Anyone can be a father, fewer become good parents.

The Beginnings

Prior to 1973, joint ventures were often "shotgun" marriages since it was

THE JOINT VENTURE

the only form of foreign investment permitted by the Japanese government. Even if an American firm had other intentions, it was forced to find a suitable bride. There were plenty to choose from. Prospective Japanese parents were eager for technology. Straight licensing agreements were preferable, but a joint venture was better than nothing.

This meant both parents really had different objectives in mind to begin the marriage, hardly an auspicious start for a new business venture. There are exceptions to this generalization, but the pattern has been so pervasive it cannot be ignored. Japanese companies were primarily interested in gaining access to new products which could be marketed by their sales forces. The joint venture was viewed as a vehicle or channel through which this could occur, hopefully at regular intervals. American companies were interested in access to the market and viewed the joint venture as a first step in the process of building a business presence in Japan.

Of course, mutually positive intentions did exist. Americans believed, both rightly and wrongly, that the joint venture offered a low-cost route of entry into a complicated market. It would be a learning experience, upon which the firm could build a respectable position. It was also cost-effective for the Japanese, as product development expenses were shared. Joint ventures provided each parent with possibilities for long-term relationships from which both could benefit.

The joint venture was, therefore, in spite of initial misgivings, entered into with much fanfare and promise for the future. Some companies were so enamored of the process that they formed several joint ventures.

In reviewing the record of joint ventures formed in Japan by all American pharmaceutical companies, several conclusions appear warranted:
1. Most major companies utilized this form of organization to enter the market.
2. Most joint ventures were formed prior to 1980, very few after that.
3. In the last decade, many joint ventures have been restructured or closed down. Usually restructuring took the form of increasing the ownership percentage of the American parent.

Joint ventures have rarely lived up to their initial promise. In retrospect, three problems are identifiable as sowing the seeds of later frustration.

Mission. The joint venture agreement, as worked out by the parents, did not provide for the step-by-step development of a company mission to perform all functions. The Japanese parent reserved for itself the function of sales and distribution. The American parent reserved for itself the right of product selection. This put the joint venture in the middle, out of touch with the basic research process at one end of the spectrum, and out of touch with its customers at the other end. Activities which it could perform were product development and registration; importation of finished material and/or a small production capacity to produce finished products; and market planning.

Being caught in the middle, the joint venture neither controlled its raw material prices nor its end selling prices. The joint venture became an expense center, not a profit center. This did not bode well for the development of a disciplined management, or one with pride in its accomplishments. Managers were reduced to messengers, shuffling back and forth between both parents asking for charity. From one, a lower product price, and from the other a greater selling effort at a high price.

The net result was a lack of responsibility and non-answers to fundamental business questions. What business are we in? Who are our customers? The answers were to come from the parents. Sometimes they did, more often they did not.

Personnel. Given a truncated mission, it is not surprising joint ventures had a difficult time creating a positive image for prospective employees. Initially, employees were transferred from the Japanese parent company under the system known as *shukkō shain*. This meant they were working in the joint venture but their home was never changed for purposes of salary scales, benefits and retirement allowances. Loyalty was not transferable under these circumstances.

Without a clear view of future viability, joint ventures could not succeed in recruiting the best employees. Secondly, in a country like Japan, in which the initial employment decision is a career decision, the joint venture was unknown to professors, family and friends. It took a great deal of courage to apply for a job in a joint venture and support for the decision was practically nonexistent.

THE JOINT VENTURE

Furthermore, in a typical Japanese company, there are many horizontal or lateral moves in the course of a career. Opportunities for this did not exist in the joint venture because it was performing a limited set of functions. Therefore, employees could not get the depth of experience their colleagues were obtaining in the fully integrated Japanese parent company.

Above all, prospective employees could easily see top management positions were not available as ultimate career options, no matter how faithfully or effectively they performed. These positions were filled with people transferred from the parent companies. The ambitious employee, while he may know it is difficult to reach the top, at least would like a shot at getting there. Also, employees realized knowledge of English was an important requirement or prerequisite for success. While this appealed to some (English language majors), it did eliminate a cadre of young people not interested in making the effort.

Top Management. The typical joint venture had a chairman or vice president from the American parent, and a president from the Japanese parent. The board of directors was made up of an equal number of people from both parents, usually not active in the joint venture. Two aspects of this structure flew in the face of conventional Japanese practices for organizing top management.

First, directors in Japanese companies are "inside" directors. They hold active management positions in the firm and have clear operational responsibilities. "Outside" directors in joint ventures could not help but treat the business as part-time, or as a baby company to be told what to do, and when to do it. Secondly, the president of a Japanese firm holds shogun-like power and the American nominated as chairman or vice president had little influence inside the company. The president was transferred from the Japanese parent and knew full well to whom he owed his loyalty. Unfortunately, these men were usually mediocre. If they had more talent they would have been kept at home in the Japanese parent company. It is difficult to identify presidents of joint venture companies with credentials on a par with those of industry leaders. Their mission was not to build. They were there to maintain a semblance of harmony and keep the ship afloat, dead in the water, but afloat.

COMMETING IN JAPAN
Lessons Worth Remembering

The joint venture is no longer considered an attractive option for either entry into the Japanese market or expansion of the business. This is not to say joint ventures are dead. Some will survive, albeit in altered form, and others will be formed. There are rational reasons to do business in Japan with a local partner beyond mere licensing of technology. Creative approaches are available to structure joint ventures which avoid or minimize the problems.

Many companies have had experiences with several joint ventures. It was not altogether a futile effort. An enormous amount of time and money was expended in managing these companies. Lessons learned are worth remembering if for no other reason than to avoid the same mistakes in the future. Several are discussed below.

Market Presence. Since no other option was legally possible, the joint venture did give American firms a presence in the market. This must be considered, on balance, as better than staying completely outside a market so large and potentially profitable as Japan. It did give American executives a degree of hands-on management experience with the peculiar and sometimes unique aspects of the market. Managers did learn the market was not as mysterious as they often had been led to believe.

Products sold by the joint venture did achieve a degree of identity related to the originator that was not possible through a straight licensing-out arrangement. Many joint ventures moved downstream by establishing sales forces to promote products directly to customers. It was discovered that promotional methods successfully utilized elsewhere were also useful in Japan. Confidence in managing a sales effort in Japan was enhanced.

Personnel. Joint ventures, in spite of inherent disadvantages, did manage to recruit, train and keep some outstanding personnel. It was demonstrated that enlightened American personnel practices were transferable to Japan. Many employees actually appreciated the less rigid environment in the joint venture. Opportunity for advancement was faster, overseas travel was possible, and merit, rather than seniority only, was included in the salary structure.

THE JOINT VENTURE

R&D. The development staff of joint ventures generally persuaded their home offices to think about the special requirements of the Japanese regulatory process early in the development cycle. This reverse flow of knowledge did make it possible to speed up development and approval in Japan. This process alone made the joint venture a valuable investment.

Production. As joint ventures integrated backward into production there was much to be learned from Japanese manufacturing methods. Using the same machines employed elsewhere, the Japanese were forever making adjustments to improve their performance. This attention to detail often provided transferable, money-saving procedures to other international operations.

Management. Many American companies did learn the value of a Japan presence beyond a token presence at board meetings. Left completely to the Japanese parent company, managers in the joint venture were muzzled, looked down upon, and reminded they were a child company. It is axiomatic that managers in the joint venture must have appropriate opportunities to grow, make decisions, and aspire to board-director positions. Imposed operational limits restricted ambition and motivation.

Organizational Structure. Many companies came to appreciate the need for a type of "corporate" presence in Japan. There are special requirements in bridging the cultural and language gaps that exist in Japan. The people who have these skills did not fit into the salary scale or personnel scheme applied to employees in a joint venture.

These bilingual, bicultural employees are more motivated if they are organizationally attached to a wholly-owned, Japan-based company. It is then possible for these employees to analyze the benefits and risks of operational decisions strictly from the standpoint of the American investor. This function cannot be effectively performed 8,000 or more miles away from the action.

The Future

Examples of successful joint ventures do exist. They have generally been able to integrate forward and backward into operations originally reserved for both parents. They have developed capable employees able to assume more and more responsibility in management.

There comes a time in the life of every joint venture when both parents must face up to the fact that they no longer have a child company. Changes must be agreed upon by both sides to permit the joint venture to operate as a fully integrated company. This may be a difficult decision and is often not possible under the best of circumstances. Nevertheless, the fact that it has been done proves it can be done.

Joint ventures, during the best and worst of times, have facilitated bringing business cultures face to face in an operating environment. Theories of joint venturing gave way to the practical realities of making a profit and running a successful business. These experiments, often failures, led to a deeper understanding of doing business in Japan.

As was noted earlier, a presence in Japan is critical for American high-tech companies. Japanese companies, on the other hand, must establish a presence in the U.S. and Europe. They are formidable competitors at home. Can they do as well abroad?

This question is relevant to American high-tech firms as they learn to compete in Japan. If they are so preoccupied with defending their home market from the onslaught of Japanese competition, there will be precious little time left to compete in Japan.

Chapter 16

JAPANESE COMPANIES AS INTERNATIONAL COMPETITORS

Japanese high-tech companies dominate their home market and prosper in a competitive environment. Increased investments in R&D are paying off with world-class products. Given no offshore presence, these products are licensed to third parties. Now companies are on the brink of international expansion. Experience in managing non-Japanese human resources is minimal. Other Japanese multinational firms have overcome this obstacle. As the inevitable unfolds, the nature of competition in other countries will be transformed.

Japanese consumer products can be found throughout the world. "Made in Japan" has become synonymous with quality, service and value. Japan's economic achievements are well known if not yet well understood. From low-tech to high-tech, Japanese products dominate many markets.

The media, stock analysts and competitors question whether pharmaceuticals will be the next wave of technological achievement to flow from Japanese shores. Which pharmaceutical companies will achieve prominence and emulate Toyota and Sony?

I believe an analysis of three key strategic factors will shed some light on these questions. The path toward internationalization is not new, it has been traveled by other companies. Annual reports of the world's twenty leading pharmaceutical companies indicate the following information for 1985 (Table 23).

TABLE 23
20 Leading Pharmaceutical Companies in 1985

Country of Origin	No. of Companies	Drugs % of Total Sales	Foreign Sales %
U.S.A.	11	49-80	22-42
Germany	3	15-85	75-80
Switzerland	3	31-61	96-98
England	2	9-82	65-97
Japan	1	57	7

As the data indicate, leading pharmaceutical companies outside Japan derive a significant portion of their corporate sales in countries other than their home base. American companies derived 34 percent of their 1986 sales from foreign countries. Swiss companies in the industry clearly had to look beyond their own small country for sales growth.

Japan, on the other hand, is a large market and has grown rapidly. This may account for the proliferation of pharmaceutical companies in Japan. A surprising fact emerges when considering the manpower scale of Japanese pharmaceutical companies, as shown in Table 24.

TABLE 24
Manpower Scale of Pharmaceutical Companies
(No.of employees)

Year	No. of Cos.	% Cos. <100	% Cos. to 1000	% Cos. >100
1975	1,359	78.7	16.5	4.8
1979	1,366	75.9	18.8	5.3
1985	1,369	72.8	20.8	6.4

JAPANESE COMPANIES AS INTERNATIONAL COMPETITORS

The number of companies has remained relatively stable, but the manpower scale has trended upward. Nevertheless, a very significant number of firms still employ less than 100 people. Given these data, many predict a reduction in the total number of companies, but there are no facts to support this view. A shake-out may come, but it will require great patience waiting for it to occur.

The size of the market, and the number of companies in the market, creates intense competition. Small companies survive in Japan but it is unlikely they will achieve the "critical mass" necessary to launch a competitive threat outside Japan.

In fact, a presence outside Japan is currently limited to less than a dozen companies, and many foreign subsidiaries of Japanese companies are not much more than listening posts staffed by a few people to monitor developments in a particular country. As might be expected, over half of the subsidiaries formed outside Japan through 1985 were in Asian countries. There are geographic, cultural and historic reasons for this investment, but these markets are not strategically important to an international business. The U.S., Japan and Europe are the critical markets.

Success at Home Leads International Expansion

The Japanese market is now approaching the size of the American market in value, although it has half the population. Many companies compete for market share, and the employee scale of most companies is small. Given these conditions, Japanese management has been preoccupied with establishing a strong base at home and has made few significant moves outside Japan.

The present situation can be characterized as follows:
1. Japanese-origin products dominate the home market and this position is not eroding (Table 25).
2. Japanese companies dominate the home market. Only four foreign-owned companies appeared in the 1987 list of twenty top companies, two American and two European.
3. The concentration ratio of the top ten companies is low (under

COMMETING IN JAPAN

TABLE 25
Market Share of Foreign-Origin and Japanese-Origin Products
(% of Total Market)

	1980	1982	1984	1986
Foreign-Origin Products	40.7	37.4	39.0	39.5
Japanese-Origin Products	59.3	62.6	61.0	60.5

40%), and no single company has more than a 6 percent share of the market.

4. The market is not concentrated in terms of a single dominant purchasing group. In 1986, there were 9,699 hospitals, but 50 percent of these had fewer than 100 beds.
5. A large marketing force is required to cover the entire range of customers. In 1985, 42 percent of the employees in Japanese companies were engaged in marketing. In the U.S., American companies have 31 percent of their employees in marketing.
6. The financial scale of the largest companies is changing. In 1975, only one company exceeded annual sales of 100 billion yen. In 1985, nine companies exceeded this level.

These statistics indicate that some Japanese companies have established a sufficiently strong base of operations in Japan to seriously consider expansion abroad.

R&D Productivity Leads International Expansion

New products have driven the growth of the high-tech drug market in Japan. The growth index for 1987 compared with 1978 stood at 195. New products launched in and after 1978 contributed 57.8 percent of this growth. Eight out of the top ten products in 1987 were launched in or after 1981.

The R&D environment in Japan can be characterized as follows:
1. The R&D expense to sales ratio has doubled during the past ten years.

2. The number of drug patents as a percent of all patents issued has doubled in the last nine years.
3. The number of R&D people in the pharmaceutical industry has doubled in the past twelve years.
4. From 1980 to 1986, the Ministry of Health and Welfare approved 267 new chemical entities for sale in Japan, 75 percent more than the number approved in the U.S. over the same time period.
5. Since 1982, on the basis of new contracts only, Japan has become a net exporter of pharmaceutical technology.
6. Japan has developed a cost-efficient, productive R&D capacity, capable of providing a flow of useful products for worldwide marketing.
7. Innovation is made in small steps, in other words, second and third-generation products. While many of these innovations have not impressed foreign regulatory authorities, they have provided opportunities for growth in market niches unfilled by foreign firms.

Management of Human Resources Outside Japan

U.S. pharmaceutical firms, on average, employ 47 percent of their people outside the U.S.; 20 percent of their R&D employees are located outside the continental U.S.

At present, the experience of Japanese firms is quite different. Only 3.3 percent of Japanese pharmaceutical sales were made outside Japan in 1985. Published data for foreign employment by Japanese firms do not exist. But judging from the number and type of foreign subsidiaries, I assume the number is under 4 percent of total employment. Virtually all Japanese R&D is conducted in Japan by Japanese employees. The conclusion is unavoidable: practically all Japanese pharmaceutical company employees are Japanese, and they live in Japan.

It naturally follows that Japanese pharmaceutical executives have had very little experience in managing either non-Japanese employees or operations outside Japan. To confirm this assumption a survey was conducted among thirteen companies in Japan. Table 26 summarizes the results.

TABLE 26
Board of Director Managerial Experience

No. of Companies	No. of Directors	R&D Experience	Foreign Country Experience
13	236	79 (33.5%)	10 (4.2%)

In retrospect, the numbers are surprise-free. Foreign country work experience parallel the level of sales outside Japan. Directors with experience in R&D parallel the increased emphasis given to research during the past decade. A similar survey done ten years ago would probably have recorded a large number of directors with experience in production. A survey done ten years from now will most likely show a larger number of directors with work experience in foreign countries.

Those Japanese firms now in offshore markets have not had serious problems managing their personnel. There is no reason to believe pharmaceutical managers will fail where others have succeeded. Although experience is limited, business ventures in Asian countries have performed satisfactorily in this regard. Japanese managers have demonstrated patience and sensitivity to local customs and personnel practices.

Future Trends

Success at home, a productive R&D effort, and lack of experience with managing non-Japanese employees characterizes the pharmaceutical industry in Japan today. Success abroad, however, may characterize the Japanese pharmaceutical industry of tomorrow.

Recent annual reports and public statements by management concentrate on the achievements in overseas markets or on plans to grow outside of Japan. It is not yet clear, however, how Japanese companies will establish their presence outside Japan. Currently, there are examples of joint ventures, equity investments, wholly-owned subsidiaries and licensing arrangements that reserve marketing rights for the Japanese firm. In short, there is no pattern; every option is being pursued in one form or another.

JAPANESE COMPANIES AS INTERNATIONAL COMPETITORS

No one has laid out a blueprint which guarantees an instant presence offshore.

The nature of a corporate structure most suitable for international expansion also remains a question mark. In the book *Thriving On Chaos, Handbook for a Management Revolution*, Tom Peters suggests that decentralization and tailoring a product to local needs is a key factor. He cites examples of U.S. firms that met with early success overseas, then rescinded the initial decentralization which contributed in unseen ways to that success.

Peters also refers to a 1980 Harvard Business Review article by Harvard's Raymond Vernon which stresses the need for a decentralized organizational structure. He quotes:

"Several factors explain the American propensity for one-way transmission (U.S. to overseas) multinational networks. Most important, (the bulk of) subsidiaries were created during a period in which U.S.-based companies characteristically had a technological lead over their competitors, generating and selling products that would represent the market of the future. As long as U.S. companies were secure in their innovative leads, there was no great need to use foreign subsidiaries as listening posts.

A second factor has been the premature obliteration of international divisions in many U.S. companies. As the foreign interests of American companies grew and flourished in the postwar period, the international divisions were often the star performers. But their success was eventually their undoing. By the middle of the 1960s, one U.S. company after another reorganized itself to acknowledge the increased importance of its foreign business. According to a study conducted in the early 1970s, the typical pattern consisted of abolishing the international division and setting up a series of so-called global product divisions to do the worrying about foreign products."

Will this experience be duplicated in Japanese companies? Actual experience in Japan is instructive. Pharmaceutical companies have given regional offices decentralized authority to act on behalf of the company in each particular geographic area. Regional directors are given substantial latitude in spending authority, and the power to respond, on the spot, to

COMMETING IN JAPAN

customer requests, rather than referring them to the home office. Managers in Asian subsidiaries are empowered to "behave in concert with local practices." In Korea, according to one source, this translates into giving promotional margins to local distributors not considered rational by American or European companies.

Japanese firms have set up international divisions and overseas subsidiaries as listening posts. How they will evolve is an unanswered question. However, if they are listening, and are able to learn from the mistakes of others, the nature of international competition will be transformed, simply because foreign companies have not experienced Japanese competition in any other market except Japan.

Other high-tech businesses have already experienced competition from Japanese competitors in international markets. Many would agree the experience is not pleasant. One answer is not to forfeit the large high-tech market in Japan to these competitors. Which brings us back to competing in Japan. The process is not mysterious or impossible. As in every competition, fundamentals apply. Those companies which master the fundamentals usually win and always gain competitive advantage.

Chapter 17

FUNDAMENTALS APPLY AS TIME GOES BY

> *American firms seeking quick fixes for their languishing growth in Japan cannot apply techniques used successfully in other markets. Unfriendly takeover bids are virtually unknown. Sales force expansion is not accomplished by placing advertisements in help wanted columns. Prices cannot be increased. Success is achieved through dedicated attention to fundamentals. Typical profit planning procedures focus attention on spending less and selling more. Front-loading expenses requires strong management commitment. Without it, mediocre performance is guaranteed.*

A market growing at double-digit rates is unforgiving to competitors who lag in committing resources to sustain a viable presence. No company is immune. American companies are not necessarily disadvantaged. A more important factor is the commitment by management to "forward spend" on fundamentals in the business.

The pharmaceutical market in Japan exemplifies the dynamic changes of a high-technology industrial sector growing at a rapid rate. During the last ten years, pharmaceutical production value in Japan has almost doubled. Value is measured at prices established by the government in the context of the National Health Insurance System. These prices are revised periodically, typically downward. As shown in Table 27, prices were dramatically lowered over a ten-year period.

TABLE 27
NHI Price Revision

Year	Type	Weighted Average % Reduction	Pharmaceutical Production (¥Billion)
1977	No Reduction		2,458.3
1978	Complete	5.8	2,793.9
1979	No Reduction		3,042.3
1980	No Reduction		3,482.2
1981	Complete	18.6	3,679.1
1982	No Reduction		3,980.2
1983	Partial	4.9	4,032.1
1984	Complete	16.6	4,027.0
1985	Partial	6.0	4,001.8
1986	Partial	5.1	4,280.7

Note: There was no price reduction in 1987 and production exceeded 5,000 billion yen.

It should also be noted that price reductions up to 1986 were either partial or complete (all products). Beginning in 1988, complete price revisions will be made every two years. In April 1988, prices were revised downward by 10.2 percent. It is an understatement to say this situation is a challenge for both Japanese and American managers.

The regulation of price in the Japanese pharmaceutical market essentially prohibits growth in revenues through price increases. In other high-tech businesses, competition may have the same impact. Management cannot enhance earnings by selectively raising prices. This factor alone gives the market a different character from the U.S., or other markets where governments permit free pricing and/or price increases. It focuses attention on increasing volume, and on a search for higher-priced new products. Executives must concentrate on:
1. Increasing usage by current customers.
2. Convincing non-users to adopt a product.

FUNDAMENTALS APPLY AS TIME GOES BY

3. Extending indications for current products.
4. Developing new product forms for current products.
5. Bringing new products to the market.

There is an insidious side to the drug pricing system. Physicians and hospitals demand discounts off the NHI price to cover their costs of dispensing drugs, and/or to generate income. The government reimburses physicians and hospitals at the NHI price level for the drugs they prescribe and dispense. The difference between purchase prices and reimbursement prices is approximately 24 percent. This represents the "doctor's margin."

By means of this system, the Japanese government has created an economic motivation for physicians to both prescribe as much as possible and buy at the largest discount. In many instances the system takes attention away from the benefits and risks of drug therapy. Physicians must query: "Is it good for me, the patient, or both of us?"

Within a firm, executives must consider the competitiveness of their discount structure, particularly for products which are not unique in a given class of therapy. In revising NHI prices, the government conducts surveys to determine actual market prices. Therefore, while a larger discount may encourage higher usage, the reimbursement price will be subject to a larger reduction at the time of a price revision.

This dilemma is unlikely to disappear in the foreseeable future. It behooves management to work toward reforms that will eliminate abuses in the system, as well as efficiently allocate health care financial resources. Several measures are being seriously debated. Nevertheless, the current system represents today's reality, which does not inherently discriminate between U.S. and Japanese manufacturers. Rather, for those who want to succeed, it puts a premium on conducting fundamental business procedures in an efficient manner. Three are worthy of consideration: product, price and people.

Product

The Japanese health insurance system, culture and infrastructure all encourage product innovation. As mentioned previously, prices of products

TABLE 28
Top Ten Pharmaceutical Products–1987

Product	Class	Sales (¥million)	Year Introduced
1. Kefral	Cephalosporin	93,646	1982
2. Krestin	Cytostatic	71,293	1977
3. Shiomarin	Cephalosporin	53,223	1982
4. Perdipine	Ca Antagonist	50,112	1981
5. Avan	Nootropics	44,831	1986
6. Adalat	Ca Antagonist	43,953	1976
7. Pansporin	Cephalosporin	40,480	1981
8. Tarivid	Quinolones	39,754	1985
9. UFT	Cytostatics	39,738	1984
10. Panaldine	Platelet Aggregation Inhibitor	37,866	1981

Note: Sales as measured by IMS and valued at the NHI price

in the market inexorably go down. The only way to achieve a higher price mix is to constantly refresh the product portfolio. Table 28 lists the top ten products in 1987. It is significant that eight out of the ten products were launched in or after 1981. Only one product was on the market over ten years.

Product line extensions are often as important to the firm as new chemical entities. Numerous examples indicate product modifications are worth pursuing for both medical and economic reasons. A dosage regimen once per day adds significant convenience and compliance value compared with three times per day. Such products also enhance volume growth. Furthermore, distinguishing a product from competitors can relieve the pressure for higher discounts, thus avoiding large price reductions.

Successful firms stress the mundane, but fundamentally important, aspects of development. New breakthroughs in drug therapy make headlines, but good development work keeps the firm competitive. Few

FUNDAMENTALS APPLY AS TIME GOES BY

can neglect basic research and stay in this business. Yet an over-emphasis on potential stars blinds a firm to contributions that can be made by innovations in formulation and chemical modification.

Development also includes the process of clearing regulatory procedures faster than competitors. This results from an in-depth knowledge of the rules and constant management attention to eliminating time-consuming roadblocks.

A Japanese company I am familiar with assigned people to the development department if they couldn't make it in sales or research. Furthermore, if there was a slowdown in the flow of products coming to development, people were moved out of the department to other positions. There was constant expansion and contraction. Employees remaining were intent on finding what was wrong with a product to justify their existence. Motivation to elucidate what was good about a product was lacking. People knew it was a dead area. Needless to say, results reflected this attitude.

American firms have often neglected the development function in their Japanese operations, relying on so-called Dev Labs located elsewhere to answer questions for the Japanese subsidiary. This approach neglects the value of intense contact with decision-makers in Japan. Products cannot be cleared by following a recipe and completing all the steps to get a seal of approval. Efforts to "harmonize" regulatory requirements between countries have made progress, but there is still no substitute for local, well-motivated expertise in this function.

Product development must also be tied closely to market development. Japanese companies have not yet learned the value of marketing. For the most part they are sales-driven, with an emphasis on how many customer calls are made in one day. Sales regions are fiefdoms, isolated from the laboratory and development department.

As time goes by, successful firms appreciate that there is more to the high-tech business than discovering or licensing a product and selling it. What happens in between is important, deserves constant attention, and has enormous payback. Management does not have the luxury of waiting for a product to fund this effort. In my experience, it is a truism that those who complain about the approval process are those who have neglected their product development department. Those who lost their competitive edge with a successful new product neglected new product forms of the original drug.

Price

A pharmaceutical product in Japan cannot be marketed unless it is listed in the National Health Insurance price list. Basically, prices are set by comparing a new product with similar products in the market. In this process, comparative clinical trials with an active drug are mandatory to demonstrate efficacy and safety.

However, this system can be abused. For example, some companies may have conducted a large-scale, expensive clinical trial to compare their drug with product X, only to be told later that the drug should have been compared with product Y. At other times, there are no rational comparative drugs. Everyone compares against the highest-priced drug on the market to guarantee a high NHI price. These anomalies should be corrected, and may be in the future. But once again, management cannot wait for the perfect system, it must operate competitively under today's rules.

Since reimbursement prices are fixed, the discount offered to customers is a critical decision. Physicians and hospitals have legitimate reasons for pressing manufacturers for a discount. The money available for covering the costs associated with dispensing drugs to patients is inadequate. To rationalize this problem, the Japanese government has promoted an idea of separating the prescribing function from the dispensing function, in other words, in an independent pharmacy.

Theoretically, the idea makes sense. Physicians receive a technical fee for their service of diagnosis. They decide what medicine a patient should receive and a pharmacy fills the prescription. However, no one has yet determined what margin is suitable for a pharmacist. Presumably the pharmacist would have less leverage over the manufacturer to demand discounts, hence rationalizing the reimbursement system.

Not much progress has been made in separating these functions, possibly because of cultural factors. People do not expect to go to another physical location for their medicine. Diagnosis and treatment are considered interrelated. At a minimum, the government should promote the separation of economic reasons for prescribing a drug from rational medical reasons.

Until all this happens, managers must play the game within the context of current rules. Some do better than others. Price decisions are not the responsibility of financial bean counters or accountants with green eyeshades. The job belongs to line-operating managers who know their customers. Organizing responsibility for pricing demands a tough cadre of people who can work with and through the distribution structure.

The management of a Japanese company believed that if their representatives created demand from physicians, wholesalers would have to follow. They remained in the comfort of their offices rather than getting out into the field to contact wholesalers and solicit their cooperation. Volume increased, but the home office did not appreciate at what price sales were made until it was too late.

Knowing your customer is a fundamental principle. It takes time and a strong stomach to meet with customers in their territory. Increasing the discount is an easy way for a manufacturer's representatives and wholesaler salesmen to generate business. This is exactly what happened to the managers mentioned above who stayed in their offices.

Training representatives is also fundamental, if for no other reason than to instill confidence. Successful Japanese companies emphasize both the time and quality of training programs. They have built separate physical facilities to train their people by professional trainers. American companies in Japan have not invested in dedicated facilities for training, probably because justifying an acceptable return on investment (ROI) was difficult.

A well-trained representative, confident in himself and his product, is much less prone to offer discounts to overcome buyer objections. Discount decisions need the focus of top management attention. Decentralization of this decision is an open invitation for price erosion. Companies with strong management have minimized discounts and downward price revisions. They have prolonged product life cycles and maintained volume growth of older products.

As in many other markets, there are both price sensitive and price insensitive customers. Targeting customers is an important part of maintaining price. It really boils down to concentration. For example, a weak company will use 150 or more wholesalers to do its business. Stronger companies concentrate on eighty wholesalers.

A Japanese CEO once told me it was better to use many wholesalers so they would compete with each other and thereby increase volume. His company's products did not represent more than 10 percent of sales in any given wholesaler in Japan. Not many wholesalers care much about companies whose full product line represents less than 10 percent of sales. Their salesmen sell on price, not performance.

American companies are now making belated moves to contact customers directly instead of forfeiting this function to Japanese companies. In many cases they will do it better than the people they relied on in the past. There is nothing "sexy" about this type of Japan strategy. But as time goes by, more companies realize that the simple formula for success in Japan is knowing your customer.

People

Nothing is more fundamental in business than people. High-tech businesses are not production-driven. Software is much more important than hardware. No one buys a high-tech company and easily realizes immediate gains from spinning off undervalued assets.

To many this may sound like apple pie and motherhood — so what else is new? Nothing is new, but many companies do not consistently hire good people, retain them and motivate them. Extraordinary accomplishments are possible by ordinary people. At times, this fundamental principle is overlooked. Managers look for "superstars," and forget about the people in the trenches.

More than one Japanese company is paralyzed by family management, which promotes people having one outstanding characteristic: loyalty to the family. They squash enterprising, entrepreneurial men because they dare to criticize the status quo.

In this regard, American companies can capitalize on policies to reward

FUNDAMENTALS APPLY AS TIME GOES BY

merit and offer a wide range of senior management positions. This is an opportunity which should not be overlooked. It is a myth that foreign companies cannot hire good people in Japan. Many successful foreign enterprises prove this to be wrong, day in and day out.

Over the years, I have talked with senior managers of many Japanese companies. CEOs of successful companies do not monopolize the conversation. Their subordinates speak freely, openly, and with animation. Less successful CEOs do not involve as many people in meetings, and those attending rarely say very much. It is easy to see beyond the myth that all Japanese look and think alike.

Companies also differ dramatically in their approach to personnel management. Successful firms send people to training programs outside the company. In these programs they are real contributors to discussions, even in an environment in which foreigners are present. Less successful companies rarely send their people outside, as though they might be contaminated by new ideas.

The basic difference is a high level of trust in the individual to act rationally and in the best interests of the company. Those without this trust delight in finding flaws in a person's character, never forgiving them, and always remembering them. People end up spying on each other, never making a decision, and sending every detail to the top of the organization. It is an insidious process.

As time goes by, it is possible to create an atmosphere in which people love to come to work. Others are attracted to the firm because they know something good is going on. Motivation is high. There is a feeling of "we can do anything." Experiencing this atmosphere makes all the books about "How to Do Business in Japan" seem trite.

The fundamental principles do apply. Nothing magical, no smoke and mirrors. Either a company has everyone believing in their own ability or they are dictating policy, keeping people bottled up, demanding blind loyalty. To believe Japanese employees respond differently to these fundamentals is to create another myth.

One factor may be different in Japan. I have often marveled at the amount of bad management employees will suffer before walking away. It may be a virtue of the culture or the stigma attached to changing jobs. At any rate, it does help to make bad managers look good.

A strong sense of obligation often contributes to prolonging the life of bad service, poor products, unreasonable price strategies, and unenlightened personnel policies. On the other hand, that same loyalty and dedication can be channeled to develop good products, and sell them well at reasonable prices.

As time passes, business people in Japan can make a choice to consistently apply well-proven, basic fundamentals to the task of building an outstanding enterprise. Those who know Japan know you get what you pay for and the costs are high. Often these costs must be incurred long before noticeable payoffs occur. Front-loading expenses are a difficult decision for a manager who expects his Japan tour to end in three years. A strong commitment is required at top corporate levels to support long-term allocation of funds.

Without this support, without a passion to succeed, and even with a dedicated, workaholic, loyal Japanese work force, the firm will be mediocre. Good products will be developed slowly, prices will erode, and good, entrepreneurial people will walk away. Scapegoats will be found for mediocre performance. Myths about the Japanese way of keeping out Americans will persist.

Today, many are proving a different scenario is a viable option. It takes time, but the rewards more than justify the effort.

Chapter 18

HIGH-TECH U.S. FIRMS CAN COMPETE

There is no alternative. High-tech U.S. firms must compete aggressively in Japan to secure respectable market share positions. If Japan is forfeited to Japanese competitors, they can operate from a protected base which frees up sizable resources for international expansion. U.S. firms will be forced into reacting versus acting. Playing defense during the entire game doesn't put many points on the scoreboard. Offensive strategies are required. Without them, managers risk competitive presence elsewhere.

In the early 1980s, it was amusing to listen to the Japan "experts" talk about what you could and could not do in Japan. I read all the books and papers that said the Japanese do not buy or sell companies because companies are people and no one would buy and sell people. They said an acquisition in Japan was not a viable corporate strategy. Company management would not permit it. Employees would oppose it. The government would never allow it to happen. Shareholders would be utterly opposed to foreign ownership.

I was amused because we were planning to do what everyone else said was impossible. During one week, in August 1983, I directed the acquisition of not one, but two Japanese-owned companies. The larger one was listed on the first section of the Tokyo Stock Exchange, a symbol of im-

165

pregnability from a takeover bid. The other, a smaller firm, was listed on the over-the-counter market, but had strong, stable shareholder support. The impossible suddenly became possible.

The government did not prevent the transactions, in fact, they processed them with amazing speed and confidentiality. Japanese management supported the moves in order to gain stronger competitive positions. The employees perceived a new and bright future. Not a single shareholder raised an objection. Japanese competitors admired our efforts.

I must admit we had planned more for failure than for the success we experienced. We were prepared to express our rationale for the purchases in exquisite, logical terms. We had arguments for every possible objection or confrontation. But we were not prepared for the question, "OK, yesterday we were a Japanese company, today we are American, now what?"

The entire matter is reminiscent of the end of World War II. One day it was assumed the Japanese would fight to the bitter end, contesting every bit of their sacred homeland. Then the late Emperor announced the war was over and the next day everyone set out to build a new, peaceful Japan. Occupation troops arrived heavily armed only to find people eager to forget the past and get on with the future.

In recent years, the so-called experts have once again brought out their crystal balls and told the world Japanese companies would not make unfriendly acquisitions in the U.S. We were informed they would be content to channel their excess liquidity into treasury bonds and other investments, where they were welcomed with open arms. Recent headlines in the business press have proved once again the "impossible" can and does occur.

The point of all this is to emphasize that nothing is impossible in Japan. Unfortunately, a lot of people make a career out of telling American businessmen what they cannot do in Japan. Many Japanese, as it suits them, join readily in this chorus of no-nos. It is not surprising that many American firms appear to be paralyzed as they evaluate their competitive position in Japan. They know they should do better, but get a bad case of whiplash when thinking about what to do.

Many employ senior Japanese managers who eloquently talk about the

HIGH-TECH U.S. FIRMS CAN COMPETE

Japanese way of doing things, which really translates into protecting their own very favorable positions. I have seen American managers agonizing over replacing an incompetent manager, fearing the effect this might have on distributors and partners. If they only realized that their Japanese partner would have taken care of this kind of situation in a very direct manner in a fraction of the same amount of time.

American managers are often intimidated by Japan because they do not know the market. They read books about how to do business in Japan and conclude that all their instincts about business need to be altered when they land in Tokyo. They go slow, readily take bad advice, and fail to commit resources to crack open the market. I am not saying what works in Indiana should be cloned in Osaka, but so many fail to notice the difference between bad advice and what it really takes to move forward.

Naturally, all this creates frustration and a desire to fight back in ways which the American manager can understand. In recent years, this has taken the form of Japan-bashing. People blame the system for being devious, unfair and discriminatory. Even the Japanese language itself is considered a non-tariff trade barrier. Various people show up at my office looking for "proof" that drugs discovered outside Japan are not approved as fast as those discovered in Japan, proof that foreign drug prices are lower and reduced more severely. When told that I know of no such proof, they go away believing I have been in Japan too long to really tell the truth.

It is an easy out to blame the "system" rather than taking a hard look in the mirror and admitting a competitor won the heart and mind of a customer; admitting you don't have the quality or quantity of people to get the job done; admitting your regulatory affairs department hardly knows the people in the Ministry of Health and Welfare; admitting you have one salesman calling on a hospital twice a week and a competitor has three people who live in the hospital every day; admitting that during the past ten years three different men were in charge of your Japanese subsidiary, and none could understand one word of a business discussion in Japanese.

The system may be a half a bubble off plum, which to my carpenter father meant unlevel. All the regulations may not be totally transparent.

COMMETING IN JAPAN

Every competitive bid may not be virgin-pure. The definition of what is fair may be debated. Abuses should be corrected. Equal access to markets should be a strong, consistent policy of our government. But at the end of the day, we must recognize the system is people, and people make judgments within an imperfect world. No one ever said life would be fair.

Many of our high-tech companies are giants in the U.S. but do not understand the rules of winning a customer in Japan. They know how to get government approvals in Washington, but not in Tokyo. The first step in any competition is to know the rules. The second is to learn the fundamentals. The third is to bring sufficient resources to bear on the opposite side. And the fourth is to be a real professional, on and off the field. American high-tech companies have products that can compete in Japan. Our quality is, or can be, as good as anything a Japanese competitor can produce. Our financial resources are adequate for the requirements of building a presence in Japan. We can attract first-rate people and motivate them to perform as well or better than the competition. We do not need to be defensive about our goals for the business.

Others have written about U.S. companies that do compete successfully in Japan. It is of interest that these firms do not complain about the rules — they have learned them. They have gone inside the system and compete aggressively.

There are U.S. managers who understand Japan and have pushed their organizations to commit resources to match the competition. They do not visit the trade office in Washington to complain about trade barriers. They know their Japanese competitors will not relax or be content with a declining market share position. They have developed a passion to compete and succeed in Japan.

Success stories are important because they dispel myths and open doors to new ways of thinking. After the four-minute mile barrier was broken it seemed like everyone could do it. Myths hinder our competitiveness in Japan. Barriers are more often imaginary than real. Many have proved it can be done. There are no excuses for the others.

BIBLIOGRAPHY

1. Abegglen, J.C. and G. Stalk, Jr., *Kaisha* (Tokyo, Charles E. Tuttle, 1985)
2. Ballon, R.J. (ed.), *Doing Business in Japan*. 2nd ed. (Tokyo, Sophia University, 1968)
3. Christopher, R.C., *Second to None—American Companies in Japan*. 1st ed. (New York, Crown Publishers, 1986)
4. Condon, J., *A Half Step Behind: Japanese Women of the '80s*. 1st ed. (New York, Dodd, Mead, 1985)
5. Drucker, P., *The Practice of Management*. (New York, Harper & Row, 1986)
6. Drucker, P., *Innovation and Entrepreneurship*. (London, Pan Books, 1985)
7. Hall, E.T., *Hidden Differences: Doing Business with the Japanese* (Garden City, N.Y., Anchor Press/Doubleday, 1987)
8. Nevis, E.C., "Cultural Assumptions and Productivity: The United States and China," *Sloan Management Review*, 1983, 24 (3), pp. 17-29.
9. Ouchi, W.C., *Theory Z: How American Business Can Meet the Japanese Challenge* (Reading, Mass., Addison-Wesley, 1981)
10. Peters, T., *Thriving on Chaos: Handbook for a Management Revolution* (New York, Knopf, Distributed by Random House, 1987)
11. Vogel, E.F., *Japan as No. One: Lessons for America* (Cambridge, Mass., Harvard University Press, 1979)
12. Van Zandt, H.F., "How to Negotiate in Japan," *Harvard Business Review* 48 (6), 1970, pp. 45-56.
13. Kokusai Shogyo Shuppan K.K., "The Actual Situation and Mid-Term Prospects of Pharmaceutical Companies." Dec. 1987.
14. Mikusu Co., Ltd., "Co-development, Co-marketing and Sales," Detailman 14 (11), Oct. 1986, pp. 22-57.
15. Yakuji Nippo, Ltd., "Questionnaire Results on Laboratories of Pharmaceutical Companies," Yakuji Nippo (Pharmaceutical News) No.7281, Nov. 12, 1987, pp. 7-13.

INDEX

Abegglen, J.C., 36-37, 56, 62
Advisory councils, 26-31; commitment toward, 27-28; procedures for, 30-31
Advisory councils, types of: business, 28-29; medical, 29; personnel, 29; scientific, 29; public relations/political, 30

Ballon, R.J., 44
Banyu Pharmaceutical Co., Ltd., 134
Blood pressure, survey results of, 35
Board of directors, union membership in, 37-38
Boston Consulting Group, 87
Business: advisory council, 28-29; statistics related to, 36-39
Business performance, reporting of, 49-50

Christopher, R.C., 39
Clinical studies, number of, 109
Co-development and co-marketing: as a growth strategy, 12; rational for, 106-113
College graduates: height and weight of, 35; life span of, 35
Condon, J., 70
Cost effectiveness of drugs, 34

Detailmen, number of, 34. *See* Medical representatives
Distribution, channels of, 129
Drucker, P., 127

Eli Lilly & Co., Inc., 58
Employees: entry level, 70; hiring of, 75; strength and weaknesses of, 70-73
Entry level employee, 76-78
Employment in the pharmaceutical industry, 66

Fair Trade Commission, 137
Family management: effect on employees, 162-163; in pharmaceutical companies, 60-61; personnel policies of, 73

Glaxo, 58
Government policies: effect on the pharmaceutical industry, 10
Group harmony and unity, 44-45; concepts of 46-47
Growth strategy, options for, 12

Hall, Edward T., 24-25
Health care: facilities, 89; personnel, 89
Health care costs: over-65 age segment, 9
Hospitals, definition of, 34; statistics related to, 33-34
Hospital market, size of, 11

Infant mortality, 85
In-house magazines, characteristics of, 46
International divisions, demise of, 153
Interpreters, weaknesses of, 17

Japan-bashing, 167
Japanese company: competitive fundamentals, 56-62; employee participation in, 51; family management of, 60-61; marketing in, 59, paternalism in, 50; presence outside Japan, 55; professional management in, 61; ranking of, 12; salary administration in, 76-77; seniority in, 50-51; unique features of, 52
Japanese language students in the U.S., 39
Japanese management, features of, 43-44
Japanese-origin products, 12
Japanese pharmaceutical market, characteristics of, 149-150
Japan presence, need for, 14
JPWA (Japanese Pharmaceutical Wholesaler Association), membership, 11
Joint venture: benefits of, 144-146; mission of, 142; personnel in, 142-143; rational

INDEX

for, 140-141; top management in, 143

Kikkoman Foods, 25

Labor disputes, number of, 38
Language barrier, 17
License agreements, characteristics of, 119
Licensing: dos and don'ts, 118; need for, 110-111; responsibility for, 117; review of candidates, 117-118
License contracts: negotiation of, 120; number of, 120-121
Lifetime employment, 45: definition of, 74, 81-82
Life expectancy at birth, 85
Life span, statistics of, 35

Market entry, options for, 12
Marketing: corporate function, 18; employees in, 71-72; of pharmaceuticals, 59
Medical advisory council, 29
Medical care, access to, 10; statistics related to, 32-35
Medical doctors employed by pharmaceutical companies, 61. *See* Physicians
Medical expenditure, by source of revenue, 89
Medical insurance, financing of, 80-81; types of, 87-88
Medical representatives: contact with customers, 59; contact with wholesalers, 59; number of, 11, 128; physician coverage by, 107-108
Marion Laboratories, 123-124
Marriage age, 35
Merck & Co., Inc., 134, 63-64: new products of, 55
Merger and acquisition, possibility of, 165-166
Mid-career employee, 78-80. *See* employee
Mortality rates, 85-87

National health insurance: claims processed, 89-90; doctor's margin in, 157; effect on wholesalers, 137; history of 84-85; pricing, 10-11, 156, 160; products in, 9
Nenko, 45
Nevis, E.C., 51
New drugs, number of, 96, 121; sales of, 99
Nissan Motor, 39

Oil shock, effect of, 28
Ouchi, W.C., 45

Patents: increase of, 115; number of, 97; restoration of, 9-10
Paternalism, 48
People, trust in, 20-21
Personnel advisory council, 29
Personnel in sales, 59-60
Peters, T., 38, 39, 153
Pharmaceutical companies: number of, 121; employment by 66; foreign sales, 148; in-house magazines, 46; manpower in, 69, 148-149
Pharmaceutical executives, experience of, 151-152
Pharmaceutical industry, 5, 68-69: family management of, 68; labor pool, 68; sales training in, 75-76
Pharmaceutical market, characteristics of, 54-55; growth of, 9; positive aspects of, 9-10; problems, 10-11; sales concentration, 11; value of, 5
Pharmaceutical production value, 156
Pharmaceutical products: pricing of, 56; top ten, 158
Pharmacy, 160-161
Physicians: access to, 10; number of, 34; visits to, 33
Physician coverage by medical representatives, 107-108
Product development: cost of, 109; importance of, 158-159; unique characteristics of, 19
Production, employees in, 71

171

INDEX

Professional management, 61
Presidents, earnings of, 37
Prices: setting of, 160; wholesale, 135; revisions, 156
Private clinic market, size of, 11
Public relations advisory council, 30

Quality, consumer expectations of, 19-20

Research, intensity of, 98-99; Japanese strengths of, 58-59; number of people in, 114; organization of, 61; risk of, 100
Research and development: characteristics of, 150-151; employees in, 71; expenditures, 5-6, 96-97, 115; facilities, 101-102; in Japanese pharmaceutical companies, 102-103
Research collaboration, 104, 111-112
Research innovation, 101
Research laboratory, 12
Research strategic alliances, 105
Retirement age, 70
Recruiting of MBA graduates, 79

Salary administration, 76
Salary based in seniority, 81
Sales training, 75-76: facilities for, 161
Scientific advisory council, 29
Senior employees, characteristics of, 80-81
Seniority, 45-46: concepts of, 48
Shukkō shain, 142
Stalk, G., 36-37, 56, 62
Stanford Business School, Sloan Program, 16-17
Stern, J., 39-40
Strategic alliances in R&D, 105
Students, time in school, 38-39
Successful companies versus unsuccessful companies, 21-22

Suggestion systems, 38
Sujō no on, 45

Tanabe Seiyaku Co., Ltd., 123-124
Technology, export of, 115-116
Trade union, characteristics of, 67

Union leaders as board directors, 37-38
Unsuccessful companies: versus successful companies, 21-22
U.S. companies: approach to wholesalers, 138-139; employee participation in, 51; employment by, 63; paternalism in, 50; poor competitive performance by, 13-14; ranking of, 6; R&D presence by, 104; seniority in, 50-51; successful characteristics of, 17-18; unique features of, 17-18
U.S. research compared to Japanese research, 4

Van Zandt, H., 45
Vernon, R., 153
Vogel, E., 38

Watson, T.J., 38
Wholesalers: approach to, 138-139; employees, 132; manufacturers' presence in, 132-134; number of, 132-133; pricing and profitability of, 135-136; consolidation of, 137-138; role of, 128-130; sales and scale of, 130-133; types of, 129-130
Women, employment of, 70
Women employees: changing attitudes of, 82; salary levels of, 78-79

Yankelovich poll, 38